NEW DIRECTIONS FOR INSTITUTIONAL RESEARCH

J. Fredericks Volkwein, *Penn State University*
EDITOR-IN-CHIEF

Evaluating Faculty Performance

Carol L. Colbeck
Pennsylvania State University

EDITOR

Number 114, Summer 2002

JOSSEY-BASS
San Francisco

EVALUATING FACULTY PERFORMANCE
Carol L. Colbeck (ed.)
New Directions for Institutional Research, no. 114
J. Fredericks Volkwein, Editor-in-Chief

New Directions for Institutional Research is indexed in *College Student Personnel Abstracts, Contents Pages in Education,* and *Current Index to Journals in Education* (ERIC).

Microfilm copies of issues and chapters are available in 16mm and 35mm, as well as microfiche in 105mm, through University Microfilms Inc., 300 North Zeeb Road, Ann Arbor, Michigan 48106-1346.

ISSN 0271-0579   electronic ISSN 1536-075X   ISBN 0-7879-6334-8

NEW DIRECTIONS FOR INSTITUTIONAL RESEARCH is part of The Jossey-Bass Higher and Adult Education Series and is published quarterly by Wiley Subscription Services, Inc., A Wiley Company, at Jossey-Bass, 989 Market Street, San Francisco, California 94103-1741 (publication number USPS 098-830). Periodicals postage paid at San Francisco, California, and at additional mailing offices. POSTMASTER: Send address changes to New Directions for Institutional Research, Jossey-Bass, 989 Market Street, San Francisco, California 94103-1741.

SUBSCRIPTIONS cost $65.00 for individuals and $125.00 for institutions, agencies, and libraries.

EDITORIAL CORRESPONDENCE should be sent to J. Fredericks Volkwein, Center for the Study of Higher Education, Penn State University, 400 Rackley Building, University Park, PA 16801-5252.

Photograph of the library by Michael Graves at San Juan Capistrano by Chad Slattery © 1984. All rights reserved.

www.josseybass.com

Printed in the United States of America on acid-free recycled paper containing at least 20 percent postconsumer waste.

CONTENTS

EDITOR'S NOTES

Forces for change within and outside academe are modifying faculty work and the way that work is—or should be—evaluated. These forces include redefinitions of faculty work roles, innovations in technology, external pressures to adopt corporate management models, and increased demands for institutional accountability.

A strong force for change emerged from The Carnegie Foundation for the Advancement of Teaching. Ernest Boyer's landmark monograph (1990) *Scholarship Reconsidered: Priorities of the Professoriate* challenged faculty and administrators to redefine academic work in terms of the four "scholarships" of discovery, integration, application, and teaching. This short monograph and its sequel, *Scholarship Assessed: Evaluation of the Professoriate* (Glassick, Huber, and Maeroff, 1997), have had profound influences on the conduct and evaluation of faculty work. Faculty work was—and often continues to be—defined by three roles: teaching, research, and service. The increasing influence of *Scholarship Reconsidered* and *Scholarship Assessed* on perceptions and evaluation of faculty work, however, pervades this volume. Seven of the nine chapters in *Evaluating Faculty Performance* cite one or both, and two chapters use the four scholarships as organizing frameworks.

Advances in computer technologies exert simultaneous internal and external pressures for change in the conduct and evaluation of faculty work. Innovative technologies are opening new opportunities for faculty to interact with constituents, colleagues, and content across all faculty roles, whether those roles are labeled teaching, research, and service or discovery, integration, application, and teaching. Technological advances also allow new methods for data collection and analysis for evaluating faculty work. Some advocates of increased use of technology in academic work also assert that faculty work roles can and should be "unbundled" in on-campus as well as virtual classrooms (Paulson, 2002). This division of labor may lead to cost savings but risks deprofessionalizing faculty as academic work becomes increasingly bureaucratized and managed by administrators rather than by academics themselves (Rhoades, 1998).

Just as technological advances, global competition, and out-moded practices spur dramatic re-creations of corporate processes, advocates for management change in higher education suggest that colleges and universities should become simultaneously more cost efficient and customer centered (Hairston, 1996). Pressures to copy corporate management practices are shaping proposed and actual changes in evaluation of faculty work. Total Quality Management and Continuous Quality Improvement may have been just administrative fads in higher education (Birnbaum, 2000), but their processes for data collection, monitoring, and assessment linger, shaping new approaches to faculty evaluation.

Concurrent with pressures to model management after private business models, public colleges and universities face increased demands for accountability to their state legislators and governing boards. In the majority of states or state systems that require performance indicators, some faculty become involved in establishing performance indicators, and all are held accountable for accomplishing those relevant to their work (Burke and Serban, 1998).

The authors of chapters in *Evaluating Faculty Performance* bring new insights to faculty work and its assessment in light of reconsideration of faculty work roles, rapid technological change, increasing bureaucratization of the core work of higher education, and public accountability for performance. This volume begins with three chapters on evaluating individual faculty work roles (teaching, research and scholarship, outreach and service) and one chapter about evaluating faculty work as an integrated whole. In Chapter One, Michael B. Paulsen provides a comprehensive yet concise review of literature on evaluating teaching and considers the reliability and validity of traditional and new evaluation tools. Paulsen's discussion of the differences between formative and summative evaluation of teaching are also relevant to evaluation of other faculty roles. After reviewing the traditional template for evaluating faculty research in Chapter Two, John M. Braxton and Marietta Del Favero consider the publication outlets and possibilities for faculty who want to disseminate the results of their scholarships of integration, application, and teaching. They suggest how to merge old and new templates for fair and mission-relevant evaluation of all aspects of faculty members' scholarly work. Marilyn Amey defines *outreach* and distinguishes it from simply being a good citizen in Chapter Three. Amey provides specific examples of evaluating faculty outreach activities and argues that adequate evaluation and recognition of outreach depend on systemic change within institutions. In Chapter Four, I assert that faculty work should be evaluated as an integrated whole and present research evidence of the ways and the extent to which some faculty integrate their work roles. I suggest how to evaluate faculty work as an integrated whole and discuss benefits of integrated evaluation for individual faculty and for the departments and institutions where they work.

The next two chapters discuss how technology in general and the World Wide Web in particular are changing faculty work and its evaluation. Craig McInnis's discussion in Chapter Five of the impact of changing technology on faculty work and its evaluation illustrates both the global impact of technology and the similarity of the challenges it brings to faculty in Australia and the United States. McInnis shows how technology may facilitate communication and decision making but add to faculty workload. He argues that technology enables greater supervision of academic work, which poses a threat to the primary source of work motivation for many academics—the autonomy to pursue their own academic interests in their own way. In Chapter Six, Robert J. Marine describes a framework for evaluating Web-based faculty work. He argues for more attention to the ways Web-work changes processes of faculty work and its outcomes.

The final three chapters illustrate practical ways that individuals, institutions, and promotion and tenure committees are using evaluations of faculty performance for career development and for departmental and institutional enhancement. Mary Taylor Huber, one of the authors of *Scholarship Assessed* (Glassick, Huber, and Maeroff, 1997), explains in Chapter Seven how national discussions about redefining scholarship are being translated into campus policies and dilemmas. Her analysis of specific faculty cases illustrates the tensions junior faculty must navigate between old and new definitions of faculty work roles as they prepare for promotion and tenure. In Chapter Eight, Michael J. Dooris provides specific examples of how institutional research faculty evaluation tools can inform decisions by central administrators and faculty senates. James S. Fairweather considers the role of faculty evaluation from the perspective of years of research about faculty work and from his own service as chair of a college reappointment, promotion, and tenure (RPT) committee. Although his primary focus is RPT, he appropriately argues that all considerations of faculty evaluation must include the growing number of non-tenure-track faculty.

Taken as a whole, the chapters in this volume contain all four elements of Boyer's scholarly domains: discovery, integration, application, and teaching. They also consider the impact of technology and accountability pressures on faculty work and its evaluation. Academic administrators, institutional researchers, and promotion and tenure committee members will find practical advice and information about processes and tools for evaluating the work of individual faculty members as well as the work of all faculty in an academic unit or institution. Individual faculty will find the information useful for preparing documentation for promotion or salary reviews.

Carol L. Colbeck
Editor

References

Birnbaum, R. "The Life Cycle of Academic Management Fads." *Journal of Higher Education*, 2000, 71(1), 1–16.

Boyer, E. *Scholarship Reconsidered: Priorities of the Professoriate.* Princeton, N.J.: The Carnegie Foundation for the Advancement of Teaching, 1990.

Burke, J. C., and Serban, A. M. (eds.). *Performance Funding for Higher Education: Fad or Trend?* New Directions for Institutional Research, no. 97. San Francisco: Jossey-Bass, 1998.

Glassick, C. E., Huber, M. T., and Maeroff, G. I. *Scholarship Assessed: Evaluation of the Professoriate.* San Francisco: Jossey-Bass, 1997.

Hairston, E. "A Picaresque Journey: Corporate Change, Technological Tidal Waves, and Webby Worldviews." *Change,* 1996, 28(2), 32–40.

Paulson, K. "Reconfiguring Faculty Roles for Virtual Settings." *Journal of Higher Education,* 2002, 73(1), 123–140.

Rhoades, G. *Managed Professionals: Unionized Faculty and Restructuring Academic Labor.* Albany: State University of New York Press, 1998.

CAROL L. COLBECK *is associate professor of higher education and a senior research associate in the Center for the Study of Higher Education, Pennsylvania State University. She conducts research on faculty integration of teaching, research, and service and on relationships between organizational climate, faculty teaching, and student learning.*

1

This chapter examines the fundamental concepts, principles, and practices that characterize the most effective of contemporary approaches to the evaluation of faculty teaching performance.

Evaluating Teaching Performance

Michael B. Paulsen

There are many comprehensive systems for the evaluation of faculty performance and guidelines for the development of such systems; each includes a substantial component devoted to evaluating faculty teaching performance (Arreola, 2000; Braskamp and Ory, 1994; Cashin, 1996; Centra, 1993; Johnson and Ryan, 2000; Richlin and Manning, 1995; Seldin, 1980, 1999a; Theall and Franklin, 1990). Contributors to this literature agree about key principles that promote effective faculty evaluation (Cashin, 1996). This chapter focuses on three principles: clarifying expectations of and by faculty, identifying the nature and sources of data to be used for evaluation, and clarifying the purposes and uses of evaluation data.

Clarifying Expectations

Clarifying the expectations that institutions and departments have for their faculty and that faculty have for their own performance are central to a successful faculty evaluation system (Arreola, 2000; Braskamp and Ory, 1994; Cashin, 1996; Seldin, 1980, 1999a). Expectations for faculty work responsibilities and outcomes are affected by institutional, departmental, disciplinary, and individual faculty priorities. These expectations also affect the methods, criteria, and the nature and sources of data used to evaluate faculty work. In recent years, both institutional and faculty expectations have begun to change because the nature of faculty work has changed. Redefinitions of faculty roles affect how the teacher role of faculty relates to the other dimensions of faculty work. Understanding long- and short-term changes in the teacher role will help clarify expectations for faculty work as a whole.

New Directions for Institutional Research, no. 114, Summer 2002   © Wiley Periodicals, Inc.

Changing Roles and Responsibilities. Teaching competes with other faculty work such as research and service in allocation of faculty time (Austin, 1996; Clark, 1987; Fairweather, 1996). However, several influential reports (for example, Bennett, 1984; Boyer, 1987, 1990; National Institute of Education, 1984) refocused institutional attention and resources on evaluation, improvement, and reward of faculty as teachers. Faculty themselves indicate they value their teaching responsibilities highly. In 1998, 72.8 percent of 33,785 faculty at 378 colleges and universities indicated that their interests were "very heavily in" or "leaning toward" teaching, while only 27.1 percent indicated the same primary interest in research (Sax, Astin, Korn, and Gilmartin, 1999). Faculty interest in teaching persists despite evidence that, across institutional types and different fields of study, faculty who spend the least time on teaching and the most on research receive the highest salaries (Fairweather, 1996).

A new multidimensional view of scholarship that embraces teaching as well as research is changing how people view and value faculty roles and responsibilities (Boyer, 1990; Hutchings and Shulman, 1999; Kreber, 2001; Kreber and Cranton, 2000; Paulsen, 2001; Paulsen and Feldman, 1995b; Rice, 1996). For example, twenty-six professional societies published discipline-specific rationales for restructuring faculty roles and responsibilities to evaluate and reward teaching in ways comparable to research (Diamond and Adam, 2000). In addition, faculty face growing expectations to create student-centered classroom learning environments, focus on active learning, use techniques of classroom assessment and research, and develop pedagogical content knowledge, even though faculty rewards are rarely linked to such teaching innovations (Lazerson, Wagener, and Shumanis, 2000).

Contextual and Flexible Expectations. An institution's mission and goals provide the framework for most discussions about expectations of and by faculty (Braskamp and Ory, 1994; Cashin, 1996; Johnson and Ryan, 2000), but institutional goals are communicated through departments. Each department has a culture with situation-specific goals, within which faculty expectations are established (Austin, 1996; Cavanagh, 1996). Disciplinary differences affect the relative emphases on teaching and research, goals of undergraduate education, perspectives on curriculum, teaching and students, teaching methods and practices, attitudes toward the improvement of teaching, students' ratings of teachers, and students' beliefs about the nature of knowledge and learning (Braxton and Hargens, 1996; Cashin, 1995; Paulsen and Wells, 1998; Smart, Feldman, and Ethington, 2000). Disciplinary differences also affect the nature and construction of pedagogical content knowledge as well as views of what constitutes effective teaching and how it should be evaluated (Hutchings and Shulman, 1999; Shulman, 1993).

Faculty and administrators should discuss expectations, particularly in department units where cultures of institutions and disciplines intersect

(Austin, 1996). An institution's goals are often implicit, and the two groups may have different perceptions of the institution's mission and the relative importance of teaching and research (Gray, Froh, and Diamond, 1992; Gray, Diamond, and Adam, 1996). Braskamp and Ory (1994) recommend, "Given the openness and dynamism of faculty work and careers, it is important that we keep expectations as dynamic and flexible as need be" (p. 59).

Faculty should be actively involved in articulating and negotiating department-specific faculty responsibilities and criteria and methods standards used to evaluate teaching (Arreola, 2000; Braskamp and Ory, 1994; Cashin, 1996; Johnson and Ryan, 2000; Richlin and Manning, 1995; Seldin, 1980, 1999a). Referring to college and university mission statements when formulating department goals will enable participants to understand how department goals relate to institutional goals. Department faculty and the chair should jointly identify the broad categories for faculty roles (teaching, research, service, academic citizenship) and articulate specific responsibilities related to each role (Cashin, 1996).

The question of what constitutes effective teaching must be addressed to identify faculty teaching responsibilities (Cashin, 1996). Careful consideration of the qualities of effective teaching is an especially important undertaking within each department context. No universally accepted definition of effective college teaching exists even though countless attempts have been made to identify the characteristics of effective teaching using a variety of theoretical perspectives and a range of qualitative and quantitative approaches.

Based on extensive consulting experience, Arreola (2000) developed a model for developing a comprehensive evaluation system by systematically collecting faculty input using worksheets and questionnaires. Faculty jointly identify the responsibilities or dimensions of their teaching role (for example, content expertise, instructional design skills, instructional delivery skills), the weight given to each dimension, the sources of information about performance on each dimension (for example, students, peers, self, chair), and the impact weight of each source for each dimension. They also identify the tool for collecting data from each source for each dimension (for example, questionnaire, review of course materials, interview, and so forth), a common rating scale, the method of computing composite weighted ratings for teaching dimensions (such as 1.25 for content expertise, 1.0 for instructional design, and 1.25 for instructional delivery), the computation of a composite weighted rating for the teaching role (1.25 + 1.0 + 1.25 = 3.5), and a minimum overall composite rating (such as 2.5).

Every faculty member should meet regularly (annually at least) with the department chair to discuss and agree on the nature of that individual's responsibilities and the methods, sources, and criteria that will be used to evaluate teaching performance (Cashin, 1996; Seldin, 1980). Faculty members should be able to focus their efforts on those activities that best match their own interests, skills, and experience by negotiating with their colleagues how they can best use their talents to contribute to the collective work of their department (Wergin and Swingen, 2000).

The Nature and Sources of Data for the Evaluation of Teaching

Multiple sources and types of data should be used to evaluate teaching. The most common sources of data are students, peers, and teachers themselves (Centra, 1993; Paulsen and Feldman, 1995a; Seldin, 1999b; Theall and Franklin, 1990).

Student Ratings. Quantitative student ratings of teaching are used more than any other method to evaluate teaching performance (Cashin, 1999; Seldin, 1999b). Student ratings play a dominant role in the operational definition of what constitutes effective teaching. Components of effective teaching identified from analysis of student ratings include six common dimensions of skill, rapport, structure, difficulty, interaction, and feedback (Cohen, 1981). Other scholars have identified from nine (Marsh, 1984) to as many as twenty-eight dimensions (Feldman, 1997).

Even though student ratings are widely used and despite the large volume of research demonstrating their validity and reliability, faculty express concerns about their meaningfulness and appropriateness. Franklin and Theall (1989) found from their survey of more than six hundred faculty and administrators at three colleges that those with greater knowledge and awareness about research on student ratings had more favorable attitudes toward the use of student ratings in teaching evaluation than those with less knowledge.

The reliability of student ratings is generally robust (Cashin, 1995; Feldman, 1977; Marsh and Dunkin, 1997). Reliability coefficients for consistency (interrater agreement) vary according to the number of students surveyed but are about .70 or higher when more than ten raters are surveyed on well-known rating forms such as the Student Instructional Report (SIR) (Centra, 1993), the Student Evaluation of Educational Quality (SEEQ) (Marsh, 1984), and the Instructional Development and Effectiveness Assessment (IDEA) (Cashin, 1995). Reliability coefficients for stability (agreement of ratings over time) are also impressive, with average correlations of .83 between student ratings at semester's end their ratings one or more years later (Marsh and Dunkin, 1997). Reliability estimates that assess the extent to which student ratings of an instructor generalize across different courses or different offerings of the same course produce coefficients of .61 and .72, respectively (Marsh, 1984). In combination, these findings indicate that for summative purposes, ratings for an instructor should be collected from an adequate number of students and should cover different courses and years (Cashin, 1999; Centra, 1993; Marsh, 1984).

The validity of student ratings is assessed by the extent to which they measure a generally agreed-upon indicator of teaching effectiveness; correlate with ratings assigned by the teachers themselves, their colleagues, administrators or alumni; or agree with qualitative student evaluations (Braskamp and Ory, 1994; Cashin, 1995; Centra, 1993; Feldman, 1989a, 1989b, 1997; Marsh and Dunkin, 1997).

Metanalyses of student ratings in for a large number of multisection courses resulted in moderate (over .30) to strong (over .50) correlations between ratings on separate dimensions and global items and student performance on common final examinations (Cohen, 1981; Feldman, 1989a). Another metanalysis (Feldman, 1989b) resulted in average correlations between student ratings and the ratings of the following other groups: alumni (.69), instructors themselves (.29), colleagues (.55), administrators (.39), and external, trained observers who had either visited instructors' classrooms or viewed videotapes of their teaching (.50). Qualitative (written or group interview) evaluations by students are highly correlated with their quantitative ratings (Braskamp and Ory, 1994). In combination, these findings provide general support for the validity of student ratings in the evaluation of teaching.

Cashin's comprehensive matrix (1989, tab. 1) indicates which sources provide data appropriate for evaluating various aspects of faculty teaching performance, thereby addressing issues of face validity. He identifies seven areas that, in combination, capture the complex concept of teaching. Four of these are appropriate for students to evaluate: delivery of instruction, assessment of instruction, availability to students, and administrative requirements.

Possible biases in student ratings must be considered, especially when ratings are to be used for summative purposes. "Bias" may be present when instructor, student, course, or administrative variables are correlated with student ratings but are "not related to teaching effectiveness" (Cashin, 1995, p. 4). Research has identified few variables that meet these conditions. Two distinctions are important. The first is the distinction between variables that are or are not related to student ratings in a way that could lead to possible bias. The second distinction is among variables related to student ratings and either appropriately related to teaching effectiveness or not.

Variables related to student ratings but not teaching effectiveness may require statistical control. They include student, course, and administrative variables. One student variable requiring control is motivation for taking courses. Students taking a course as an elective tend to give higher ratings than those taking a course as a requirement (Feldman, 1978). A student's expected grade is also correlated with student ratings of instructors (Feldman, 1976). Expert evaluators disagree about whether grading leniency in conjunction with workload does or does not bias student ratings (Greenwald and Gillmore, 1997a, 1997b; Marsh, 1984; Marsh and Dunkin, 1997; Marsh and Roche, 2000).

Several course variables are related to student ratings. Students tend to rate graduate and upper-division courses higher than undergraduate and lower-division courses, respectively. Students rate courses in the arts and humanities somewhat higher than in the social sciences, which in turn, are rated higher than math and science courses (Cashin, 1995; Feldman, 1978; Marsh, 1984; Marsh and Dunkin, 1997). If faculty and administrators observe that students rate differently by level of course, academic field, or motivation for taking the course and if they suspect that such differences may be due to differences in the characteristics of the students or courses and not to differences in the effectiveness of the teachers, then normative or comparative groups should be established to promote greater fairness in the comparison of ratings (Cashin, 1995, 1999). Finally, student ratings tend to be higher in relation to the following administrative factors: when the instructor is present, when students know the purpose is for personnel decisions, and when forms are not anonymous (Braskamp and Ory, 1994; Centra, 1993). These issues can be controlled by using standardized instructions to students regarding the purposes of the ratings, asking students not to sign their names, and requiring instructors to leave the classroom while forms are completed (Cashin 1995, 1999).

Peer Review of Teaching. Although many experts agree that students are qualified to assess many aspects of classroom teaching (for example, clarity of presentation, interpersonal rapport with students, concern for students progress), they also assert that for some aspects of teaching (mastery of content, course goals, course organization and materials), only peers have the substantive expertise required for meaningful evaluation (Cashin, 1989; Chism, 1999; Hutchings, 1996b). In short, peer review brings content-based contextuality to evaluation of teaching.

Specialists in teaching and its evaluation also agree that the work of an individual faculty member is valued more when it has been subjected to rigorous peer review (Cavanagh, 1996; Chism, 1999; Diamond and Adam, 2000; Hutchings, 1996a, 1996b). Therefore, research is more highly valued than teaching (Boyer, 1990). Faculty expect public review of the methods and products of their research. In contrast, methods and products of teaching are rarely discussed or shared with peers. Just as the quality of research improves due to dialogue and debate among disciplinary peers, so would the quality of teaching benefit from similar opportunities (Boyer, 1990; Chism, 1999; Hutchings, 1996a, 1996b).

Proponents of peer review of teaching acknowledge a set of key issues and concerns, including privacy of the reviewed, needs of the reviewer, and reliability and validity of the ratings. What goes on in the classroom has traditionally been between teachers and their students, not between teachers and their peers. Peer review challenges norms of privacy by opening doors to classrooms and making teaching a public act (Chism, 1999; Hutchings, 1996a). Ending "pedagogical solitude" may be uncomfortable for many faculty (Shulman, 1993). Yet faculty are sharing many stories of successful experiments with peer collaboration and peer review (Hutchings, 1996a; Langsam and Dubois, 1996; Nordstrom, 1995; Quinlan, 1996). These changes bring increasing opportunities for new faculty to be mentored in ways that socialize them to peer collaboration and review (Hutchings and Shulman, 1999), and they may promote a culture of collaboration and community surrounding teaching (Cavanagh, 1996; Hutchings, 1996a, 1996b).

Reviewers' concerns must also be considered (Cavanagh, 1996; Chism, 1999, DeZure, 1999; Hutchings, 1996a, 1996b; Seldin, 1980). Without careful planning, peer reviewers could be placed in awkward situations when asked to judge a colleague, wrestle with issues of confidentiality, risk lack of anonymity, assess the strengths or weaknesses of a senior colleague, worry about potential ambiguous legal issues, and devote time and energy to matters that they may not perceive to be part of their job (Centra, 1993; Chism, 1999; Hutchings, 1996a, 1996b).

The reliability and validity of peer ratings of teaching are not as well established as they are for student ratings. Classroom observations of teaching have been used in a growing number of institutions (Seldin, 1999b). Research has indicated that, in the absence of either sound training or adequate numbers of observers, peer ratings based *solely* on classroom observation are not generally reliable (Centra, 1993). Questions of validity arise about whether the presence of an obtrusive observer might alter classroom behavior (Cohen and McKeachie, 1980). But there is general consensus that training in the observation of classroom teaching and that increasing the number of observers and the number of visits they make to each class would, in combination, increase the reliability of peer classroom observation to acceptable levels (Braskamp and Ory, 1994; Centra, 1993; Chism, 1999; DeZure, 1999). Departments using peer observation to evaluate classroom teaching should follow sound procedures in selecting and training observers; identifying the number of observers and number and length of classroom visits; collecting data to use in assessing the reliability and validity of observers and observations; establishing guidelines, criteria, and standards for observation; developing forms and methods for making observations; and preparing the report of the observations (Chism, 1999; DeZure, 1999).

Studies of general peer ratings of overall teaching effectiveness have produced reliability estimates ranging from .64 to .86 (Cohen and McKeachie, 1980). Kremer (1990) found that reliability across all peer raters was only .50, but when only those raters who indicated that they had high confidence in their rating were considered, reliability estimates increased to .82. Correlations with student ratings have ranged from .62 to .87. Feldman's metanalysis (1989b), based on some studies that did and some that did not include classroom observations, resulted in an average correlation with student ratings of .55. The correlations between student and peer ratings may be somewhat overstated because one of the likely bases for peers' ratings were previous ratings of students available to them—that is, the two sets of ratings may not be entirely independent (Cohen and McKeachie, 1980; Feldman, 1989b; Marsh and Dunkin, 1997).

What are peer reviewers best qualified to evaluate? Peer review should be used to provide data on aspects of teaching effectiveness for which faculty peers are the best available source of information (Arreola and Aleamoni, 1990; French-Lazovik, 1981), including expertise in the subject matter and discipline-specific aspects of instructional design and pedagogy (Arreola, 2000; Chism, 1999; Shulman, 1993). Five areas appropriate for peer review are subject matter mastery, curriculum development, course design, delivery of instruction, and assessment of instruction (Cashin, 1989). Only peers can evaluate the first three, whereas both peers and students can evaluate the last two.

Self-Evaluation or Report: Peer Review of the Teaching Portfolio. Although self-evaluations by teachers lack the validity and objectivity necessary for summative evaluation (Centra, 1993), support is growing for the use of teaching portfolios with data supplied by the instructor (Arreola, 2000; Braskamp and Ory, 1994; Centra, 2000; Chism, 1999; Seldin, 1993). "Course syllabi and exams" and "self-evaluation or report" were among the fastest-growing sources of data used in evaluating teaching performance between 1988 and 1998 (Seldin, 1999b, p. 14). The expanding use of these data sources is consistent with the nationwide increase in the use of peer review of portfolios to evaluate faculty teaching performance.

Research on reliability of peer review of teaching portfolios appears promising. In one study, faculty elected a six-member executive committee to evaluate all faculty dossiers in the areas of research, teaching, and service (Root, 1987). The composite reliability coefficients for the six raters were .97, .90, and .90 for research, teaching, and service, respectively. In a study of peer review of teaching portfolios for summative purposes at a community college, faculty wrote personal statements and provided descriptions, examples, and other documentation of their teaching effectiveness on thirteen aspects of teaching arranged into three categories: motivational skills, interpersonal skills, and intellectual skills (Centra, 1993, 1994). Each portfolio was evaluated by a dean, one peer selected by the instructor, and another peer designated by the dean. The ratings by the dean and the peer designated by the dean (peer B) were significantly correlated with each other and with student ratings; however, the ratings of the peer selected by the instructor (peer A) were not significantly related to those of the other raters.

Several steps can enhance the reliability and validity of peer ratings of teaching portfolios in summative evaluation (Centra, 1993, 1994, 2000; Root, 1987). First, portfolios should include a broad range of work samples and related information to document various aspects of teaching performance. Second, peer reviewers should receive training that includes opportunities to discuss methods, criteria, and standards for assessment using portfolios that have previously been rated high or low. Third, peers' objectivity as reviewers will be enhanced if they are not being currently evaluated and if they are selected by the unit head, randomly selected, or elected to a peer committee on teaching. Fourth, a minimum of three and a maximum of six peer reviewers should be used.

Reliability of peer ratings of portfolios would also be enhanced if a set of mandated items were included in every portfolio. Seldin (1993) recommends the following items: a reflective statement about the instructor's teaching approach, three years' of summaries of student ratings, three years' of syllabi for all courses taught, innovative course materials, and evidence of activities to improve one's teaching. Chism's sourcebook on peer review provides other models and detailed guidance (Chism, 1999).

Purposes and Uses of Evaluation Data

Evidence on teaching effectiveness can be collected for two uses—formative and summative (Braskamp and Ory, 1994; Centra, 1993; Marsh and Dunkin, 1997; Paulsen and Feldman, 1995a; Theall and Franklin, 1990). The purpose of formative evaluation is to provide informative feedback to assist faculty in improving the effectiveness of their teaching. The purpose of summative evaluation is to provide information to assist department chairs, faculty committees, and deans in making personnel decisions related to hiring, renewing or terminating faculty, awarding tenure, promotion, and merit pay increases.

To address these different purposes effectively, different types of information may be needed from the evaluation system (Abrami and d'Apollonia, 1990; Arreola and Aleamoni, 1990; Cashin, 1999; Theall and Franklin, 1990). For developmental purposes, the evaluation system should generate regularly collected and detailed diagnostic data that can be confidentially provided to individual teachers to help them identify strengths and weaknesses in their teaching behavior, establish priorities, and plan strategies for teaching improvement. Detailed diagnostic data may not be essential or appropriate for summative purposes. Instead, evaluation may be based on summary data from multiple sources of a teacher's overall teaching performance in more than one course over an extended period of time. However, the relationship between formative and summative evaluation is no less important than the distinction between them. If evaluation data and procedures are used for formative (developmental) purposes prior to being used for summative purposes (judgment), faculty have opportunities to become more familiar with the nature of the data, methods, and criteria that will be for subsequent summative evaluation of their teaching. As a result, they can strive to improve their performance before it is formally assessed (Centra, 1993). Hutchings (1996a) makes a strong argument for bridging the summative-formative distinction. When faculty are successful in making teaching community property and when they construct a culture of collaboration and peer review around teaching, they will have attitudes and perform actions that could serve both summative and formative purposes well. This bridging already happens with research (Hutchings, 1996a). Even advanced and experienced researchers deliberately seek formative evaluation (informative feedback) from peers to help improve the quality of their research work. They seek feedback, knowing very well that their peers are also likely to judge their research performance in summative ways, such as reviewing abstracts for conference presentations, manuscripts submitted for publication, or proposals for funded research or such as serving as external reviewers for tenure, promotion, or awards. In their roles as researchers, faculty bridge the formative-summative distinction without hesitation or concern. Perhaps soon, the distinction between summative and formative evaluation of teaching will no longer be useful or meaningful, because teaching will have become community property, just as research has been for so many years.

Summary

This chapter examined concepts, principles, and practices of effective contemporary approaches for evaluating faculty teaching performance. The chapter included elements of comprehensive systems for the evaluation of teaching performance, including faculty roles and responsibilities, criteria and methods for evaluating faculty performance. Next, the sources, types, reliability and validity of data used for evaluation, including student ratings, peer review, self-report and portfolios, were examined in some depth. The roles of rewards, disciplinary perspectives, and institutional teaching cultures in the development of effective teaching evaluation systems were considered from a variety of perspectives. Finally, the distinctions and relationships between formative and summative evaluation were discussed from philosophical, conceptual, and practical perspectives.

References

Abrami, P. C., and d'Apollonia, S. "The Dimensionality of Ratings and Their Use in Personnel Decisions." In M. Theall and J. Franklin (eds.), *Student Ratings of Instruction: Issues for Improving Practice.* New Directions for Teaching and Learning, no. 43. San Francisco: Jossey-Bass, 1990.

Aleamoni, L. M. "Student Rating Myths Versus Research Facts: An Update." *Journal of Personnel Evaluation in Education,* 1999, 13(2), 153–166.

Arreola, R. *Developing a Comprehensive Faculty Evaluation System: A Handbook for College Faculty and Administrators on Designing and Operating a Comprehensive Faculty Evaluation System.* Bolton, Mass.: Anker, 2000.

Arreola, R., and Aleamoni, L. "Practical Issues in Designing and Operating a Faculty Evaluation System." In M. Theall and J. Franklin (eds.), *Student Ratings of Instruction: Issues for Improving Practice.* New Directions for Teaching and Learning, no. 43. San Francisco: Jossey-Bass, 1990.

Austin, A. "Institutional and Departmental Cultures: The Relationship Between Teaching and Research." In J. Braxton (ed.), *Faculty Teaching and Research: Is There a Conflict?* New Directions for Institutional Research, no. 90. San Francisco: Jossey-Bass, 1996.

Batista, E. "The Place of Colleague Evaluation in the Appraisal of College Teaching: A Review of the Literature." *Research in Higher Education,* 1976, *4,* 257–271.

Bennett, W. J. *To Reclaim a Legacy.* Washington, D.C.: National Endowment for the Humanities, 1984.

Boyer, E. L. *College: The Undergraduate Experience in America.* New York: Harper and Row, 1987.

Boyer, E. L. *Scholarship Reconsidered: Priorities of the Professoriate.* Princeton, N.J.: The Carnegie Foundation for the Advancement of Teaching, 1990.

Braskamp, L. A., and Ory, J. C. *Assessing Faculty Work: Enhancing Individual and Institutional Performance.* San Francisco: Jossey-Bass, 1994.

Braxton, J., and Hargens, L. "Variation Among Academic Disciplines: Analytical Frameworks and Research." In J. Smart (ed.), *Higher Education: Handbook of Theory and Research.* Vol. 11. New York: Agathon Press, 1996.

Cashin, W. E. *Defining and Evaluating College Teaching.* Idea Paper, no. 21. Manhattan, Kans.: Center for Faculty Evaluation and Faculty Development, Kansas State University, 1989.

Cashin, W. E. *Student Ratings of Teaching: The Research Revisited.* Idea Paper, no. 32. Manhattan, Kans.: Center for Faculty Evaluation and Faculty Development, Kansas State University, 1995.

Cashin, W. E. *Developing an Effective Faculty Evaluation System.* Idea Paper, no. 33. Manhattan, Kans.: Center for Faculty Evaluation and Faculty Development, Kansas State University, 1996.

Cashin, W. E. "Student Ratings of Teaching: Uses and Misuses." In P. Seldin (ed.), *Current Practices in Evaluating Teaching: A Practical Guide to Improved Faculty Performance and Promotion/Tenure Decisions.* Bolton, Mass.: Anker, 1999.

Cavanagh, R. R. "Summative and Formative Evaluation in the Faculty Peer Review of Teaching." *Innovative Higher Education,* 1996, *20*(4), 235–240.

Centra, J. A. *Reflective Faculty Evaluation: Enhancing Teaching and Determining Faculty Effectiveness.* San Francisco: Jossey-Bass, 1993.

Centra, J. A. "The Use of the Teaching Portfolio and Student Evaluations for Summative Evaluation." *The Journal of Higher Education,* 1994, *65*(5), 555–570.

Centra, J. A. "Evaluating the Teaching Portfolio: A Role for Colleagues." In K. E. Ryan (ed.), *Evaluating Teaching in Higher Education: A Vision for the Future.* New Directions for Teaching and Learning, no. 83. San Francisco: Jossey-Bass, 2000.

Chism, N. *Peer Review of Teaching: A Sourcebook.* Bolton, Mass.: Anker, 1999.

Clark, B. R. *The Academic Life: Small Worlds, Different Worlds.* Princeton, N.J.: The Carnegie Foundation for the Advancement of Teaching, 1987.

Cohen, P. A. "Student Ratings of Instruction and Student Achievement: A Meta-analysis of Multisection Validity Studies." *Review of Educational Research,* 1981, *51*(3), 281–309.

Cohen, P. A., and McKeachie, W. J. "The Role of Colleagues in the Evaluation of College Teaching." *Improving College and University Teaching,* 1980, *28*(4), 147–154.

DeZure, D. "Evaluating Teaching Through Peer Classroom Observation." In P. Seldin (ed.), *Current Practices in Evaluating Teaching: A Practical Guide to Improved Faculty Performance and Promotion/Tenure Decisions.* Bolton, Mass.: Anker, 1999.

Diamond, R. M., and Adam, B. E. (eds.). *The Disciplines Speak II: More Statements on Rewarding the Scholarly, Professional, and Creative Work of Faculty.* Washington, D.C.: American Association for Higher Education, 2000.

Fairweather, J. S. *Faculty Work and Public Trust: Restoring the Value of Teaching and Public Service in American Academic Life.* Boston: Allyn & Bacon, 1996.

Feldman, K. A. "Grades and College Students' Evaluations of Their Courses and Teachers." *Research in Higher Education,* 1976, *4,* 69–111.

Feldman, K. A. "Consistency and Variability Among College Students in Rating Their Teachers and Courses: A Review and Analysis." *Research in Higher Education,* 1977, *6*(3), 223–274.

Feldman, K. A. "Course Characteristics and College Students' Ratings of Their Teachers." *Research in Higher Education,* 1978, *9,* 199–242.

Feldman, K. A. "The Association Between Student Ratings of Specific Instructional Dimensions and Student Achievement." *Research in Higher Education,* 1989a, *30*(6), 583–645.

Feldman, K. A. "Instructional Effectiveness of College Teachers as Judged by Teachers Themselves, Current and Former Students, Colleagues, Administrators, and External (Neutral) Observers." *Research in Higher Education,* 1989b, *30*(2), 113–135.

Feldman, K. A. "Identifying Exemplary Teachers and Teaching: Evidence from Student Ratings." In R. Perry and J. Smart (eds.), *Effective Teaching in Higher Education: Research and Practice.* New York: Agathon Press, 1997.

Franklin, J., and Theall, M. "Who Reads Ratings: Knowledge, Attitudes, and Practices of Users of Student Ratings of Instruction." Paper presented at the annual meeting of the American Educational Research Association, San Francisco, Apr. 1989.

French-Lazovik, G. "Peer Review: Documentary Evidence in the Evaluation of Teaching." In J. Millman (ed.), *Handbook of Teacher Evaluation.* Beverly Hills: Sage, 1981.

Gray, P. J., Diamond, R. M., and Adam, B. E. *A National Study on the Relative Importance of Research and Undergraduate Teaching at Colleges and Universities.* Syracuse, N.Y.: Center for Instructional Development, Syracuse University, 1996.

Gray, P. J., Froh, R. C., and Diamond, R. M. *A National Study of Research Universities on the Balance Between Research and Undergraduate Teaching.* Syracuse, N.Y.: Center for Instructional Development, Syracuse University, 1992.

Greenwald, A. G., and Gillmore, G. M. "Grading Leniency Is a Removable Contaminant of Student Ratings." *American Psychologist,* 1997a, *52*(11), 1209–1217.

Greenwald, A. G., and Gillmore, G. M. "No Pain, No Gain? The Importance of Measuring Course Workload in Student Ratings of Instruction." *Journal of Educational Psychology,* 1997b, *89*(4), 743–751.

Hutchings, P. *Making Teaching Community Property: A Menu for Peer Collaboration and Peer Review.* Washington, D.C.: American Association for Higher Education, 1996a.

Hutchings, P. "The Peer Review of Teaching: Progress, Issues and Prospects." *Innovative Higher Education,* 1996b, *20*(4), 221–234.

Hutchings, P., and Shulman, L. "The Scholarship of Teaching: New Elaborations, New Developments." *Change,* 1999, *31*(5), 11–15.

Johnson, T., and Ryan, K. "A Comprehensive Approach to the Evaluation of College Teaching." In K. E. Ryan (ed.), *Evaluating Teaching in Higher Education: A Vision for the Future.* New Directions for Teaching and Learning, no. 83. San Francisco: Jossey-Bass, 2000.

Kreber, C. (ed.). *Scholarship Revisited: Defining and Implementing the Scholarship of Teaching.* New Directions for Teaching and Learning, no. 86. San Francisco: Jossey-Bass, 2001.

Kreber, C., and Cranton, P. "Exploring the Scholarship of Teaching." *Journal of Higher Education,* 2000, *71*(4), 476–495.

Kremer, J. F. "Construct Validity of Multiple Measures in Teaching, Research, and Service and Reliability of Peer Ratings." *Journal of Educational Psychology,* 1990, *82*(2), 213–218.

Langsam, D. M., and Dubois, P. L. "Can Nightmares Become Sweet Dreams? Peer Review in the Wake of a Systemwide Administrative Mandate." *Innovative Higher Education,* 1996, *20*(4), 249–259.

Lazerson, M., Wagener, U., and Shumanis, N. "Teaching and Learning in Higher Education, 1980–2000." *Change,* 2000, *32*(3), 13–19.

Marsh, H. W. "Students' Evaluations of University Teaching: Dimensionality, Reliability, Validity, Potential Biases, and Utility." *Journal of Educational Psychology,* 1984, *76,* 707–754.

Marsh, H. W., and Dunkin, M. J. "Students' Evaluations of University Teaching: A Multidimensional Perspective." In R. Perry and J. Smart (eds.), *Effective Teaching in Higher Education: Research and Practice.* New York: Agathon Press, 1997.

Marsh, H. W., and Roche, L. A. "Effects of Grading Leniency and Low Workload on Students' Evaluations of Teaching: Popular Myth, Bias, Validity, or Innocent Bystanders?" *Journal of Educational Psychology,* 2000, *92*(1), 202–228.

National Institute of Education. *Involvement in Learning: Realizing the Potential of American Higher Education.* Washington, D.C.: U.S. Government Printing Office, 1984.

Nordstrom, K. "Multiple-Purpose Use of a Peer Review of Course Instruction Program in a Multidisciplinary University Department." *Journal on Excellence in College Teaching,* 1995, *6*(3), 125–144.

Paulsen, M. B. "The Relation Between Research and the Scholarship of Teaching." In C. Kreber, (ed.), *Scholarship Revisited: Defining and Implementing the Scholarship of Teaching.* New Directions for Teaching and Learning, no. 86. San Francisco: Jossey-Bass, 2001.

Paulsen, M. B., and Feldman, K. A. *Taking Teaching Seriously: Meeting the Challenge of Instructional Improvement.* ASHE-ERIC Higher Education Report, no. 6. Washington, D.C.: Association for the Study of Higher Education, 1995a.

Paulsen, M. B., and Feldman, K. A. "Toward a Reconceptualization of Scholarship: A Human Action System with Functional Imperatives." *The Journal of Higher Education,* 1995b, *66*(6), 615–640.

Paulsen, M. B., and Wells, C. "Domain Differences in the Epistemological Beliefs of College Students." *Research in Higher Education,* 1998, *39*(4), 365–384.

Quinlan, K. M. "Involving Peers in the Evaluation and Improvement of Teaching: A Menu of Strategies." *Innovative Higher Education,* 1996, *20*(4), 299–307.

Rice, R. E. *Making a Place for the New American Scholar.* Washington, D.C.: American Association for Higher Education, 1996.

Richlin, L., and Manning, B. "Evaluating College and University Teaching: Principles and Decisions for Designing a Workable System." *Journal on Excellence in College Teaching,* 1995, *6*(3), 3–15.

Root, L. S. "Faculty Evaluation: Reliability of Peer Assessments of Research, Teaching, and Service." *Research in Higher Education,* 1987, *26*(1), 71–84.

Sax, L., Astin, A., Korn, W., and Gilmartin, S. *The American College Teacher.* Los Angeles: Higher Education Research Institute, UCLA, 1999.

Seldin, P. *Successful Faculty Evaluation Programs.* Crugers, N.Y.: Coventry Press, 1980.

Seldin, P. *Successful Use of Teaching Portfolios.* Bolton, Mass.: Anker, 1993.

Seldin, P. "Building Successful Teaching Evaluation Programs." In P. Seldin (ed.), *Current Practices in Evaluating Teaching: A Practical Guide to Improved Faculty Performance and Promotion/Tenure Decisions.* Bolton, Mass.: Anker, 1999a.

Seldin, P. "Current Practices—Good and Bad—Nationally." In P. Seldin (ed.), *Current Practices in Evaluating Teaching: A Practical Guide to Improved Faculty Performance and Promotion/Tenure Decisions.* Bolton, Mass.: Anker, 1999b.

Shulman, L. S. "Teaching as Community Property: Putting an End to Pedagogical Solitude." *Change,* 1993, *25*(6), 6–7.

Smart, J., Feldman, K., and Ethington, C. *Academic Disciplines: Holland's Theory and the Study of College Students and Faculty.* Nashville, Tenn.: Vanderbilt University Press, 2000.

Theall, M., and Franklin, J. "Student Ratings in the Context of Complex Evaluation Systems." In M. Theall and J. Franklin (eds.), *Student Ratings of Instruction: Issues for Improving Practice.* New Directions for Teaching and Learning, no. 43. San Francisco: Jossey-Bass, 1990.

Theall, M., and Franklin, J. (eds.). *Effective Practices for Improving Teaching.* New Directions for Teaching and Learning, no. 48. San Francisco: Jossey-Bass, 1991.

Weimer, M. *Improving College Teaching.* San Francisco: Jossey-Bass, 1990.

Wergin, J. F., and Swingen, J. N. *Departmental Assessment: How Some Campuses Are Effectively Evaluating the Collective Work of Faculty.* Washington, D.C.: American Association for Higher Education, 2000.

MICHAEL B. PAULSEN is professor of education and coordinator of graduate studies in higher education in the department of educational leadership, counseling, and foundations at the University of New Orleans.

2

This chapter considers the limitations of traditional faculty assessment systems in the context of Boyer's four domains of scholarship and suggests a new organizing template for realigning assessment systems to accommodate work in all four domains.

Evaluating Scholarship Performance: Traditional and Emergent Assessment Templates

John M. Braxton and Marietta Del Favero

In *Scholarship Reconsidered: Priorities for the Professoriate*, Boyer (1990) asserted that the definition of *scholarship* should expand to include the scholarships of discovery, application, integration, and teaching. The most standard form of scholarship is discovery, acquiring knowledge for its own sake through testing and generating theory. Applying disciplinary knowledge and skill to societal problems characterizes the scholarship of application, whereas the scholarship of integration involves making meaning from research findings. The scholarship of teaching involves continuous examination of pedagogical practices (Boyer, 1990).

Boyer provides several reasons for expanding the boundaries of scholarship to include these four domains. First, the faculty reward structure fails to correspond to the full range of daily scholarly activities performed by faculty. The majority (59 percent) of college and university faculty have published five or fewer articles in refereed journals during their careers (Boyer, 1990). Such faculty are neither unscholarly nor unproductive (Blackburn, 1974; Braxton and Toombs, 1982). Expanding the parameters of what counts as scholarship would better reflect the scholarly activities of members of the professoriate who seldom or never publish. Second, the missions of most colleges and universities fail to acknowledge the forms of scholarship most congruent with their missions. Currently, the research university model, with its heavy emphasis on discovery, provides an inappropriate yardstick for measuring scholarly attainments at the full range of colleges and universities (Boyer, 1990; Ladd, 1979). Third, scholarship should be useful for solving pressing social and economic problems.

Glassick, Huber, and Maeroff (1997) write, "It's one thing to give scholarship a larger meaning, but the real issue revolves around how to assess other forms of scholarship" (p. 21). We concur. In this chapter, we address issues related to the appraisal of Boyer's four domains of scholarship. We first describe traditional approaches to faculty assessment, then explore how they fit with Boyer's domains, and finally examine how publication outlets vary in number and impact across several disciplines for the scholarships of discovery, application, and teaching.

Traditional Approach to Faculty Assessment

Faculty scholarly performance has traditionally been assessed by "straight counts" (Lindsey, 1980) of publications, such as articles in refereed journals, books, monographs, book chapters, and presentations at professional meetings (Braskamp and Ory, 1994; Centra, 1993; Miller, 1987, 1972; Braxton and Bayer, 1986; Seldin, 1985). Such straight counts, however, require weights to make comparisons between types of publications. Braxton and Bayer (1986) caution that disciplines may vary in the weight ascribed to different types of publications. In so-called soft or low-consensus disciplines such as sociology, psychology, political science (Biglan, 1973; Braxton and Hargens, 1996), original scholarly books and monographs are often weighted more heavily than journal articles, textbooks are weighted more than edited books, and edited books receive equivalent weight to articles published in high-quality journals. In so-called hard or high-consensus disciplines such as biology, chemistry, and physics, journal articles might receive more weight than books.

Qualitative appraisals of publications include distinctions between refereed and nonrefereed journals, journal quality ratings, indices of the contribution made by a publication, or a book publisher's reputation (Braxton and Bayer, 1986; Centra, 1993). Because an article in a refereed journal has been assessed and certified by experts in the field as making a contribution to knowledge, it may be considered of higher quality than an article in a nonrefereed journal (Braxton and Bayer, 1986). Refereed journals also vary in quality. Each academic discipline has core journals that scholars rate more highly than other journals. The impact factor for a journal is another indicator of quality (Braxton and Bayer, 1986; Gordon, 1982; McDonough, 1975; Smart and Elton, 1981). The average number of citations received for each article published in the focal journal provides the basis for the calculation of the impact score for a given journal (Smart, 1983).

Traditional Template and Domains of Scholarship

In this section, we describe publication forms for each of the four scholarship domains from an inventory of scholarly activities developed by Braxton and others (2000). The forms of scholarship included in this inventory were identified through the writings of Boyer (1990), Braxton and Toombs (1982), and Pellino, Blackburn, and Boberg (1984). We also consider the appropriateness of the traditional template for assessing Boyer's four domains of scholarship.

Publication forms pertinent to the *scholarship of discovery* include a refereed journal article, a book, or a book chapter describing a new theory developed by the author and a refereed journal article or a book reporting findings of research designed to gain new knowledge. The traditional publication-assessment template poses few problems for the appraisal of these forms of publications.

The following forms of publications associated with the *scholarship of application* fit the traditional template for assessing faculty scholarship: an article that reports the findings of research designed to solve a practical problem, an article that outlines a new research problem identified through the application of the knowledge and skill of one's academic discipline to a practical problem, an article that describes new knowledge obtained through the application of the knowledge and skill of one's academic discipline to a practical problem, an article that applies new disciplinary knowledge to a practical problem, and an article that proposes an approach to the bridging of theory and practice.

Disciplinary differences arise, however, when considering the appropriateness of the traditional template for assessing the scholarship of application. Some academic disciplines are *pure* in their research activities, whereas others are *applied* in their research orientation (Biglan, 1973). Faculty members from pure academic disciplines may be at a disadvantage if they wish to engage in the scholarship of application and publish the outcomes. This would be true if journals associated with applied academic disciplines are more likely to publish articles about application than journals in pure disciplines, if applied fields have more journals that focus primarily on the scholarship of application than pure disciplines, or if books that address application from applied disciplines are more likely to be published by scholarly presses than such articles from pure disciplines.

The use of journal impact scores based on citations counts may also be problematic for qualitative assessments of publications associated with the scholarship of application. Journal impact scores are well suited for the scholarship of discovery as an indicator of quality because of its emphasis on advancements in knowledge and the development of theory. Citations indicate recognition of contributions to knowledge, as scholars acknowledge intellectual debts to others. Citations to the work of scholars engaged in the scholarship of application may be less frequent because of the nature of the knowledge base developed through applied scholarship. As a consequence, journal impact scores may be inappropriate indices of quality of publications pertinent to the scholarship of application.

The fit between publication of *scholarship of integration* and the traditional template for scholarship assessment is problematic, although some integration publication forms fit the traditional template. They include a review of literature on a disciplinary or interdisciplinary topic, an article or book chapter on the application of a research method or theory borrowed from another academic discipline to one's own discipline, an article or book that crosses subject matter areas, a textbook, and an edited book.

Some academic disciplines may have more publication outlets for the scholarship of integration than others. Faculty members in soft fields, such as history and sociology, publish more integration scholarship than do their counterparts in hard disciplines, such as biology and chemistry (Braxton and others, 2000). Therefore, citation rates for scholarship of integration publications may vary between hard and soft disciplines.

Some publication forms that result from the scholarship of integration fail to correspond to the traditional template for scholarship appraisal, including a review essay of two or more books on similar topics, a critical book review, an article or book addressing current disciplinary or interdisciplinary topics published in the popular press, and a book published reporting research findings to the lay reader. Faculty tenure and promotion committees, academic deans, chief academic affairs officers, and college and university presidents should consider whether these publication forms should be considered measures of publication productivity in the scholarship of integration. Such deliberations might include discussion of the relationship between institutional missions and the contribution of such publications to the welfare of the lay public.

Scholarship of teaching publications that appear to be optimum fits with the traditional scholarship assessment template are those that report a new teaching approach or instructional method developed by the author. Other publication forms reflecting the scholarship of teaching include a publication listing resource materials for a course; a publication on examples, materials, class exercises, or assignments that help students to learn difficult course concepts; a publication on an approach or strategy for dealing with class-management problems faced in teaching a particular type of course; a publication on an approach or strategy to help students to think critically about course concepts; a publication of methods to make ungraded assessments of student learning of course content; and a publication on the use of a new instructional practice and the alterations made to make it successful. These various publication forms might be journal articles, books, or book chapters.

Applying the traditional scholarship assessment template to these forms of publication raises two important issues. One is whether there are many journals or university and commercial presses that publish scholarship related to teaching in various academic disciplines. Another issue concerns the rate of citation to articles appearing in teaching journals. Because such articles are most likely to make contributions to practice, citations to such articles may be so infrequent that citation rates cannot be used as an indicator of quality.

Assessing the Fit Between the Traditional Template and Boyer's Domains

As described in the previous section, the traditional template for assessing faculty scholarship has relied upon the number of publications, the form of publications, and the prestige afforded the publication outlet. Consistent with Glassick, Huber, and Maeroff (1997), Fiddler and others (1996), Diamond (1993), Froh, Gray, and Lambert (1993), and Seldin (1991), we argue that the traditional publication-assessment template is not appropriate for evaluating quality across Boyer's four scholarship domains. In this section, we analyze data from the *Journal Citation Reports* of the *Sciences Citation Index* (Institute for Scientific Information, 1999a) and the *Social Sciences Citation Index* (Institute for Scientific Information, 1999b) to address the question, To what extent do publication outlets across disciplines vary in number and impact for the scholarships of discovery, application, integration, and teaching?

Methods. We examined the journal impact factor, as an objective measure of quality or prestige of journals in selected disciplines. The journal impact factor measures the frequency with which the "average article" in a journal has been cited in a particular year (Institute for Scientific Information, 1999a, 1999b). It is calculated by dividing the number of current citations to articles published in the two previous years by the total number of articles published in the two previous years The likelihood that any piece of scholarly work will be cited more than once is low; the modal number of lifetime citations to any single scholarly work is either zero or one (Braxton and Bayer, 1986). Citation rates can be expected to vary among disciplines and among subspecialties within disciplines. The Institute for Scientific Information's (ISI) *Journal Citation Reports* (1999a, 1999b) indicates that citation information provides a "systematic, objective way to determine the relative importance of journals within their subject categories." The potential attractiveness of a particular journal as a publication outlet can thus be determined using aggregated citation data, or the journal impact factor.

We examined journal impact scores from hard-pure disciplines (chemistry and physics), hard-applied disciplines (engineering and computer science), and psychology, a soft-pure discipline (Biglan, 1973). The journals in these disciplines were laid out in the ISI journal database in a way that best allowed for subjective judgment about the form of scholarship published. For example, journals in psychology were grouped into nine categories that included applied psychology, a category apparently dedicated to the scholarship of application. Categorical groupings of journals in soft-applied disciplines such as education or business did not lend themselves to this type of analysis. Several disciplines, however, have journals devoted to teaching as evidenced by journal titles. This group of journals offers evidence of publication outlets for the scholarship of teaching.

Maximum impact factor scores for discipline subject categories, sorted from the highest to lowest score for each category, are presented in Table 2.1. Journal categories numbered six in chemistry, ten in physics, ten in psychology, thirteen in engineering, and seven in computer science.

Journal Outlets for Applied Scholarship. In hard-pure disciplines, journal categories featuring application have low impact scores. The impact factor scores for chemistry indicate that journals that publish applied scholarship in chemistry are considered less important than those that publish pure scholarship of discovery. Applied chemistry journals as a group, with a maximum journal impact score of 3.85, rank in sixth, or last, place amongst all chemistry journals, while medicinal chemistry journals, another applied area, with a score of 4.37, rank fifth. In contrast, journals in the physical chemistry category have the highest maximum impact factor score of 15.52, and the categories of organic and of inorganic and nuclear, each with a maximum score of 10.10, follow.

There is a similar pattern in physics. Rankings of physics journals place astrophysics, biophysics, and condensed matter physics, with maximum impact factors of 15.07, 13.56, and 13.44, respectively, of highest importance. Applied, mathematical, and robotics are of least importance, with maximum impact factors of 4.85, 2.05, and 1.66, respectively. The three core knowledge areas of engineering—chemical (6.67), electrical (5.36), and mechanical (4.90)—reflect the highest maximum impact scores.

Maximum impact scores for psychology's ten journal subject categories range from a low of 1.65 for mathematical psychology to a high of 11.28 for biological psychology. Again, journals focusing on applied scholarship rank ninth with a score of 2.04, perhaps reflecting the lesser importance of application than of core content areas such as experimental psychology (6.91), social psychology (6.91), and developmental psychology (6.29).

Journal Outlets for the Scholarship of Teaching. The ISI database included a journal subject category entitled Education in Scientific Disciplines (see Table 2.1). This grouping included such journals as *Academic Medicine, Journal of Chemical Education,* and *American Journal of Pharmaceutical Education.* The maximum impact factor score for this group is 1.47, a low score compared to journals focused on other forms of scholarship. For example, the engineering journal *IEEE Transactions on Education* carries an impact factor score of 0.313, lower than all engineering journal subject categories, which range from 0.83 to 6.67. Similarly, the score for the *Journal of Chemical Education* is 0.56, while the maximum scores in other chemistry journal subject categories range from 3.85 to 15.52.

In addition, we reviewed journals listed in the *Social Science Citation Index* to identify those devoted to teaching in soft-applied and soft-pure consensus disciplines. As reflected in Table 2.2, we identified nine journals in the disciplines of communication, social work, nursing, economics, sociology, psychology, law, and anthropology. Impact scores were generally low and ranged from 0.26 for *Anthropology and Education Quarterly* to 0.64 for the *Journal of Social Work Education.*

Table 2.1. Journal Impact Factor Scores for Selected Disciplines.

Journal Subject Category[a]	Number of Journals	Maximum Impact Score	Score Distribution								
			<1	<2	<3	<4	<5	<6	<7	<8	8+
Hard-Pure											
Chemistry, physical	90	15.52	—	—	—	—	—	—	—	—	—
Chemistry, organic	48	10.10	22	9	8	4	3	—	—	—	1
Chemistry, inorganic and nuclear	37	10.10	15	9	4	2	2	1	1	—	2
Chemistry, analytical	66	6.75	27	24	9	2	2	—	1	—	—
Chemistry, medicinal	30	4.37	9	13	3	2	2	—	—	—	—
Chemistry, applied	49	3.85	33	13	1	1	—	—	—	—	—
Astronomy/Astrophysics	36	15.07	17	6	9	1	1	1	—	—	1
Biophysics	55	13.56	17	13	10	6	3	2	—	2	2
Physics, condensed matter	54	13.44	23	24	2	1	1	—	—	—	2
Physics, nuclear	21	7.67	5	7	6	1	—	1	—	1	—
Physics, particles/fields	18	6.87	5	6	2	3	—	1	1	—	—
Physics, atomic/molecular/chemical	31	6.67	7	12	7	1	1	1	1	—	—
Physics, fluids/plasma	19	5.60	8	5	5	—	—	1	—	—	—
Physics, applied	67	4.85	35	26	3	—	3	—	—	—	—
Physics, mathematical	25	2.05	12	11	2	—	—	—	—	—	—
Robotics/Auto control	48	1.66	44	4	—	—	—	—	—	—	—
Multidisciplinary sciences[b]	52	29.49	41	7	1	—	—	—	—	—	3
Hard-Applied											
Engineering, chemical	110	6.67	90	19	—	—	—	—	1	—	—
Engineering, electrical/electronic	205	5.36	157	37	8	2	—	1	—	—	—
Engineering, mechanical	98	4.90	89	5	1	—	1	—	—	—	—
Engineering, environmental	36	3.75	28	5	1	1	—	—	—	—	—
Engineering, biomedical	43	2.98	26	14	3	—	—	—	—	—	—
Engineering, civil	62	1.44	58	4	—	—	—	—	—	—	—
Engineering, petroleum	27	1.42	26	1	—	—	—	—	—	—	—
Constructive/Building, technology	26	1.22	25	1	—	—	—	—	—	—	—
Engineering, industrial	31	1.13	29	2	—	—	—	—	—	—	—
Engineering, marine	20	1.07	19	1	—	—	—	—	—	—	—
Engineering, geological	17	1.00	16	1	—	—	—	—	—	—	—
Engineering, manufacturing	33	0.95	33	—	—	—	—	—	—	—	—
Aerospace engineering/technology	26	0.83	26	—	—	—	—	—	—	—	—
Computer science, interdisciplinary applications	76	4.21	62	7	5	—	1	—	—	—	—
Computer science, artificial intelligence	63	2.83	46	13	4	—	—	—	—	—	—
Computer science, software, graphics, programming	67	2.70	54	12	1	—	—	—	—	—	—
Computer science, theory and methods	61	2.70	51	9	1	—	—	—	—	—	—
Computer science, information systems	62	2.55	45	12	4	—	—	—	—	—	—
Computer science, hardware architecture	45	1.96	34	10	—	—	—	—	—	—	—
Computer science, cybernetics	18	1.85	16	2	—	—	—	—	—	—	—
Soft-Pure											
Psychology, biological	15	11.28	3	10	—	1	—	—	—	—	1
Psychology	107	7.79	76	19	4	3	—	—	2	2	—
Psychology, experimental	64	6.91	24	26	6	3	2	1	1	—	—
Psychology, social	41	6.91	30	8	2	—	—	—	—	—	—
Psychology, developmental	48	6.29	24	15	5	2	—	—	1	—	—
Psychology, clinical	87	4.17	58	22	2	4	1	—	—	—	—
Psychology, educational	38	3.24	27	9	2	—	—	—	—	—	—

Table 2.1. (continued)

Journal Subject Category[a]	Number of Journals	Maximum Impact Score	Score Distribution							
			<1	<2	<3	<4	<5	<6	<7	<8 8+
Soft-Pure (continued)										
Psychology, psychoanalysis	13	2.26	11	1	1	—	—	—	—	— —
Psychology, applied	49	2.04	34	14	1	—	—	—	—	— —
Psychology, mathematical	10	1.65	9	1	—	—	—	—	—	— —
Sociology	97	3.48	82	12	1	2	—	—	—	— —
Political science	76	2.12	66	9	1	—	—	—	—	— —
History	16	1.57	15	1	—	—	—	—	—	— —
Soft-Applied										
Education in scientific disciplines	13	1.47	12	1	—	—	—	—	—	— —

Note: Journal impact factor: A measure of the frequency with which the "average article" in a journal has been cited in a particular year; used for assessing a journal's relative importance, particularly in relation to other journals in the same field.

[a]Individual journals may be included in more than one subject category.

[b]Because this was a category in the *Sciences Citation Index*, it is assumed to include hard sciences fields.

Journal Outlets for the Scholarship of Integration. Because the scholarship of integration is often multi- and interdisciplinary (Glassick, Huber, and Maeroff, 1997; Boyer, 1990), more possibilities may exist for journal publications as a scholar could access journals in more than one discipline. The journal impact score data offers some interesting information about publication of integration scholarship. The journal subject category "multidisciplinary sciences" (see Table 2.1) reflects a maximum journal impact score of 29.29—almost twice the magnitude of the highest score in the hard sciences. In addition, this subject category has three journals with impact scores of 8 or above, more than any other subject category. This suggests the potential attractiveness of multidisciplinary journals as an outlet for the scholarship of integration in the hard sciences. Further, interdisciplinary applications journals, with a maximum score of 4.21, ranked first in the computer science journal categories, suggesting the high level of importance attributed to integrative publication outlets in that field.

Disciplinary Comparisons. Journals from hard disciplines have higher impact scores than journals from soft disciplines. This suggests that scholars in these disciplines may have more attractive journal outlets for presentation of their scholarship. With the exception of psychology, soft disciplines do not demonstrate similar impact. For example, sociology journals reflected a maximum impact score of 3.48, and political science and history journals had scores of 2.12 and 1.57, respectively (see Table 2.1). Such a comparison supports assertions that scholars in hard disciplines tend toward journal publications, while soft discipline scholars publish more books (Braxton and Hargens, 1996). Our analysis of journal impact data suggests that the comparatively low level of importance attributed to journals in soft disciplines may be a factor in disciplinary differences in use of journals as publication outlets.

Table 2.2.   Journals on Teaching in the Disciplines.

Journal Name	Impact Factor
Journal of Social Work Education	0.64
Communication Education	0.62
Journal of Economic Education	0.51
Teaching Sociology	0.50
Nursing Education Today	0.44
Teaching of Psychology	0.30
Journal of Nursing Education	0.29
Journal of Legal Education	0.27
Anthropology and Education Quarterly	0.26

Limitations of Traditional Template: Conclusion. This analysis of journal impact also illustrates that the traditional template for measuring quality of scholarly work does not accommodate all scholarship forms. Tenure and promotion review policies should consider disciplinary differences in terms of the importance attributed to the various journal subject categories. These varying levels of importance suggest that faculty at many types of institutions may produce scholarship for publication outlets that have not traditionally been afforded high status. Disciplinary affiliation may moderate this tendency.

There is some evidence that journal publication outlets available to scholars in pure and applied disciplines may vary. Within a single discipline, journals focusing on applied scholarship are generally attributed lesser importance as measured by journal impact scores, which translates for the individual scholar into a publication of lesser prestige. There is also evidence that teaching-focused journals are not readily available to faculty in all disciplines who want to publish about the scholarship of teaching. Only nine journals of this type were identified in soft disciplines. Although thirteen teaching-focused journals were listed for hard disciplines, the level of importance attributed to these journals was low enough to make them less attractive as a publication outlet.

Assessing quality of scholarly work outside the discovery domain poses challenging issues. Just as experts and critics are calling for a "fresher, more capacious vision of scholarship" (Boyer, 1990, p. 9), traditional assessment approaches should be reexamined to develop new templates that will accommodate scholarly work in the integration, application, and teaching domains.

Toward a New Template for the Assessment of Scholarly Activities

As previously indicated, the current faculty reward structure fails to correspond to the day-to-day scholarly activities of those members of the professoriate who seldom or never publish. Moreover, this predominant reward structure rests on the application of the traditional template for scholarship assessment. To align the reward structure with the scholarly efforts of faculty who seldom or never publish, activities reflecting scholarships of application, integration, and teaching should be taken into account in the tenure and promotion process. The assessment of scholarship as a set of activities requires a new organizing template. Components of this template might include:

1. Activities submitted as indices of scholarships of application, integration, or teaching should be public, amenable to critical review, and accessible for exchange and use by other members of the scholarly community (Shulman, 1999). Thus, they should be in observable form, such as papers, presentations, reports, videos, computer software, and Web sites. Presentations should be audio- or videotaped so they are observable to those unable to attend a presentation.

2. Indices of scholarship performance in the domains of application, integration, or teaching should be assessed using six criteria: clear goals, adequate preparation, appropriate methods, significant results, effective presentation, and reflective critique (Glassick, Huber, and Maeroff, 1997). Clear goals, adequate preparation, and appropriate methods assess the *quality* of a given scholarly activity. The principle index of the quality of an activity, however, is the contribution it makes to the academic discipline, colleagues at other colleges and universities, the lay public, or students. The traditional scholarship template assesses contributions using citations to published work and letters from peers at other universities commenting on the contributions of a faculty member's publications. The contribution made by other scholarly activities will require the development of some new assessment approaches.

3. Indices of scholarship performance should be accompanied by documentation. Portfolios of "application," "integration," or "teaching" should be developed by candidates for tenure or promotion (Glassick, Huber, and Maeroff, 1997; Froh, Gray, and Lambert, 1993). Such documentation provides the basis for peer assessment of scholarly activities using the six criteria delineated by Glassick, Huber, and Maeroff (1997). Portfolios should include the scholar's statement of responsibilities, a biographical sketch, and selected samples of scholarly activities and should outline the scholar's goals in engaging in the scholarly activities they have performed. The scholar should characterize the nature of each activity as befitting one of Boyer's domains of scholarship and should describe the contributions made by selected portfolio examples and by their total body of scholarly activities. In addition, the scholar might also describe plans for future scholarly engagement, how the various activities fit together to form a coherent program of scholarly activity, and how the scholarly activities meet the mission of the department or institution (Glassick, Huber, and Maeroff, 1997).

The biographical sketch takes the form of a curriculum vita that should list the activities performed by the scholar. The form of the activity that makes it observable by others—presentation, report, paper, video—should also be indicated. With the use of such a curriculum vita, the scholarship of candidates using scholarly activities can be quantitatively assessed (Glassick, Huber, and Maeroff, 1997), or straight counted, as are books, book chapters, monographs, and journal articles.

The portfolio should also contain samples of a candidate's scholarly activities that are referenced and described in the candidate's statement of personal responsibility. Samples of scholarship should be easy to assess using the six criteria delineated by Glassick, Huber, and Maeroff (1997) and make significant and easily identifiable contributions.

Braxton and others (2000) provide examples of scholarly activities that might be included in such documentation. Activities from the *scholarship of application* include studies conducted for a local organization, a local nonacademic professional association, or a local governmental agency to help solve a community, county, or state-level problem. Examples reflecting the *scholarship of integration* include talks on a multidisciplinary topic given on a local radio station, a local television station, before a local business organization, or before a local or a nonacademic professional association. Developing examples, materials, class exercises, or assignments that help students to learn difficult course concepts, strategies for dealing with class-management problems faced in teaching a particular type of course, approaches to help students to think critically about course concepts, and methods to make ungraded assessments of student learning of course content are examples of activities associated with the *scholarship of teaching.* All of the preceding activities must be in a form observable by others.

Concluding Reflections

The use of Boyer's domains of scholarship requires approaches for assessing faculty scholarship performance that incorporate the traditional template and new templates for scholarship. Institutional research officers, faculty tenure and promotion committees, academic deans, and chief academic affairs officers should attend to the following issues.

The publicly observable scholarly activities of faculty who seldom publish should be given some weight in the tenure and promotion process. However, publications in the form of journal articles, book chapters, monographs, and books reap the greatest rewards and are valued the most by the academic profession (Braxton and Toombs, 1982; Ladd, 1979; Boyer, 1990). As a consequence, it seems reasonable that individuals who seldom publish should be expected to have a few publications resulting from their engagement in the scholarships of application, integration, and teaching that appear in the form of a journal article, book chapter, book, or monograph. The threshold number of such publications needs serious consideration by faculty promotion and tenure committees, academic deans, and chief academic affairs officers. Institutional research officers should contribute to this discussion by compiling data on prevailing publication productivity norms at peer colleges and universities.

Quantitative assessments constitute a dimension of the traditional template for scholarship assessment. The role quantitative assessments play in assessing publicly observable scholarly application, integration, and teaching requires deliberation. Some straight counting of such scholarly activities should occur. However, the threshold number of such activities needs to be carefully considered by faculty tenure and promotion committees, academic deans, and chief academic affairs officers. These deliberations should take into account types of scholarship most congruent with the mission of a given college and university. Institutional research officers should collect data from peer institutions on quantitative expectations for scholarly activities that are publicly observable but not published as a book, book chapter, monograph, or journal article.

Boyer's call to expand the boundaries of the definition of scholarship holds much promise for the realignment of institutional missions and faculty reward systems. Without careful consideration and development of assessment approaches, such realignments will fail to occur. The formulations of this chapter are presented to help make progress toward this end.

References

Biglan, A. "The Characteristics of Subject Matter in Different Academic Areas." *Journal of Applied Psychology,* 1973, *58,* 195–203.

Blackburn, R. T. "The Meaning of Work in Academia." In J. I. Doi (ed.), *Assessing Faculty Efforts.* San Francisco: Jossey-Bass, 1974.

Boyer, E. L. *Scholarship Reconsidered: Priorities of the Professoriate.* Princeton, N.J.: The Carnegie Foundation for the Advancement of Teaching, 1990.

Braskamp, L. A., and Ory, J. C. *Assessing Faculty Work: Enhancing Individual and Institutional Performance.* San Francisco: Jossey-Bass, 1994.

Braxton, J. M., and Bayer, A. E. "Assessing Faculty Scholarly Performance." In J. W. Creswell (ed.), *Measuring Faculty Research Performance.* New Directions for Institutional Research, no. 50. San Francisco: Jossey-Bass, 1986.

Braxton, J. M., and Hargens, L. L. "Variations Among Academic Disciplines: Analytical Frameworks and Research." *Higher Education: Handbook of Theory and Research.* Vol. 11. New York: Agathon Press, 1996.

Braxton, J. M., and Toombs, W. "Faculty Uses of Doctoral Training: Consideration of a Technique for the Differentiation of Scholarly Effort from Research Activity." *Research in Higher Education,* 1982, *16*(3), 265–286.

Braxton, J. M., and others. "The Institutionalization of Boyer's Four Domains of Scholarship." Paper presented at the Annual Meeting of the Association for the Study of Higher Education, Sacramento, Calif., Nov. 2000.

Centra, J. A. *Reflective Faculty Evaluation: Enhancing Teaching and Determining Faculty Effectiveness.* San Francisco: Jossey-Bass, 1993.

Diamond, R. M. "Instituting Change in the Faculty Reward System." In R. M. Diamond and B. E. Adam (eds.), *Recognizing Faculty Work: Reward Systems for the Year 2000.* New Directions for Higher Education, no. 81. San Francisco: Jossey-Bass, 1993.

Fiddler, M., and others. "Broadening the Scope of Scholarship: A Suggested Framework." *Innovative Higher Education*, 1996, *21*(2), 127–139.

Froh, R. C., Gray, P. J., and Lambert, L. M. "Representing Faculty Work: The Professional Portfolio." In R. M. Diamond and B. E. Adam (eds.), *Recognizing Faculty Work: Reward Systems for the Year 2000*. New Directions for Higher Education, no. 81. San Francisco: Jossey-Bass, 1993.

Glassick, C. E., Huber, M. T., and Maeroff, G. I. *Scholarship Assessed: Evaluation of the Professoriate*. San Francisco: Jossey-Bass, 1997.

Gordon, M. D. "Citation Rankings Versus Subjective Evaluation in the Determination of Journal Hierarchies in the Social Sciences." *Journal of the American Society for Information Science*, 1982, *33*, 55–57.

Institute for Scientific Information. *Journal Citation Reports: Sciences Citation Index*. [http://jcr.isihost.com]. 1999a.

Institute for Scientific Information. *Journal Citation Reports: Social Sciences Citation Index*. [http://jcr.isihost.com]. 1999b.

Ladd, E. C. "The Work Experience of American College Professors: Some Data and an Argument." *Current Issues in Higher Education*, 1979, *2*(3), 13.

Lindsey, D. "Production and Citation Measures in the Sociology of Science: The Problem of Multiple Authorships." *Social Studies of Science*, 1980, *10*, 145–162.

McDonough, C. C. "The Relative Quality of Economics Journals Revisited." *Quarterly Review of Economics and Business*, 1975, *15*, 91–97.

Miller, R. I. *Evaluating Faculty Performance*. San Francisco: Jossey-Bass, 1972.

Miller, R. I. *Evaluating Faculty for Promotion and Tenure*. San Francisco: Jossey-Bass, 1987.

Pellino, G. R., Blackburn, R. T., and Boberg, A. L. "The Dimensions of Academic Scholarship: Faculty and Administrator Views." *Research in Higher Education*, 1984, *20*(1), 103–115.

Seldin, P. *Changing Practices in Faculty Evaluation*. San Francisco: Jossey-Bass, 1985.

Seldin, P. *The Teaching Portfolio*. Bolton, Mass.: Anker, 1991.

Shulman, L. S. "Taking Teaching Seriously." *Change*, 1999, *31*(4), 10–17.

Smart, J. C. "Stability of Educational Journal Characteristics: 1977–1980." *Research in Higher Education*, 1983, *19*, 285–293.

Smart, J. C., and Elton, C. F. "Structural Characteristics and Citation Rates of Education Journals." *American Educational Research Journal*, 1981, *18*, 399–413.

JOHN M. BRAXTON *is professor of education in the higher education administration program at Peabody College, Vanderbilt University. His research on the professoriate concentrates on differentiating and explaining faculty teaching and scholarly role performance, the normative structure of teaching and research, academic discipline differences, and the relationship between teaching and research.*

MARIETTA DEL FAVERO *is an assistant professor in Louisiana State University's department of educational leadership, research, and counseling and received her Ph.D. in education and human development from Vanderbilt University. Her research focuses on faculty and administrative work, disciplinary variations in academic leadership behaviors, and the social structures embedded in academic leadership contexts.*

3

Systemic reform is necessary to allow for an acceptance of and emphasis on outreach performance as an area of faculty work critical to faculty and institutional growth and development.

Evaluating Outreach Performance

Marilyn J. Amey

Outreach has long been an area of faculty work for which meaningful evaluation processes are lacking. Often considered consulting or service activity, most institutions have not dealt constructively with ways to acknowledge, evaluate, and reward outreach activity. Yet, what do we do with faculty work that does not fit into traditionally narrow definitions of teaching and research? Are these aspects of faculty work just part of being a good citizen? Is being a good citizen and taking one's turn on sundry college committees the same thing as providing discipline-based expertise to the larger institution in addressing a serious faculty, student, or learning problem? Is becoming involved in one's local community organizations as a volunteer the same thing as providing professionally grounded expertise in working with those outside the walls of academe on a field-based problem? With or without expectations that each faculty member engages in such activities, the category "service" is commonly used to accommodate this broad mix. Those committed to a different organizational orientation for postsecondary institutions suggest that it is time to seriously consider using new labels and creating acceptable procedures to evaluate professionally grounded faculty work that may fall outside of—or weave through—the traditional tripartite of teaching, research, and service (Boyer, 1990; Edgerton, 1993; Fear and Sandmann, 1997; Ramaley, 2000; Votruba, 1997). They call for emphasizing faculty outreach performance as critical to individual faculty development and to appropriate positioning of colleges and universities in the twenty-first century.

Understanding Outreach Contexts and Definitions

In the last decade, many scholars and administrators have called for the reprioritization of faculty work; for new definitions of teaching, research, and service; and for repositioning academic work in the future. No work

NEW DIRECTIONS FOR INSTITUTIONAL RESEARCH, no. 114, Summer 2002 © Wiley Periodicals, Inc.

resonated so much with faculty and administrators as Boyer's *Scholarship Reconsidered* (1990), Barr and Tagg's "From Teaching to Learning" (1995), and Eugene Rice's *Making a Place for the New American Scholar* (1996). These works articulate the need for fundamental changes in the ways faculty engage intellectually with others, whether the engagement is called teaching, research, scholarship, service, or outreach.

These scholarly calls to arms, contrasted with postsecondary institutions' calls to service common in the 1990s, suggest a different environment for personnel policy, decision making, and faculty role enactment. The definitions and means by which colleges and universities meet the calls to service vary. No longer are colleges and universities the only educational service deliverers. Even in the midst of competition from nontraditional providers for the role of educating the populace, postsecondary institutions are being pressed to be good citizens in the community (broadly defined) and to assist with economic and community development (Ramaley, 2000). Public sentiment is growing that universities should inform problem-solving processes through responsible extension and application of academic expertise (for example, outreach), rather than solving problems themselves (Votruba, 1997). This may involve assisting with economic development to improve global competitiveness, improving the quality of K–12 education, or overcoming public costs of urban and rural poverty. Ramaley (2000) characterizes the shift from fixer to change collaborator as "engagement," or sharing activities that have mutual consequences.

How faculty teaching and research reconnect the institutional mission to the knowledge needs of society, what many call "outreach," is a central challenge of postsecondary education today (Fear and Sandmann, 1997; Votruba, 1997; Ramaley, 2000). When faculty use their scholarship expertise to meet the knowledge needs of others and fulfill institutional mission, outreach takes place (Fear and Sandmann, 1997; Lynton, 1995; Schon, 1995; Votruba, 1997). Defined this way, outreach cuts across teaching, research, and service and involves institutional and unit-related activity for the direct benefit of external audiences: generating, transmitting, applying, and preserving knowledge. Examples of outreach performance include technical assistance, policy analysis, program evaluation, organizational development, community development, service learning, program development, expert testimony, impact evaluations, noncredit instruction, and technology transfer (Lynton, 1995; Votruba, 1997). To be considered outreach, these activities must be grounded in current knowledge of the field and result in direct benefits for external constituents and new insights for the field (Votruba, 1997). They should involve service to a community while raising important issues whose investigation may lead to generalizations applicable for others (Schon, 1995). Outreach work is serious and demanding, requiring the rigor and the accountability traditionally associated with research activities (Boyer, 1990) and, consequently, is very different from just being a good citizen.

In the 1990s, the professional development school movement and ser-vice learning were early examples of newly defined outreach initiatives that integrated faculty work into the knowledge needs of society. Then, as now, few sound institutional processes and structures supported this kind of work. Faculty engaged in activities that did not fit the discrete categories of teaching, research, and service; that extended beyond a single academic year (and, therefore, faculty evaluation cycle); and for which there were not accepted forms of evaluation. These problems notwithstanding, fac-ulty work with professional development schools and service learning combined professional education, research, and continuing professional development around community-based problems and was grounded in mutually beneficial problem solving (Ramaley, 2000). Similar examples of outreach are found in health education centers in health care professions, clinical practice sites in social services, and university-industry partner-ships in engineering and science fields. These sustainable partnerships typ-ically yield fruitful results for all concerned. Without sound evaluation systems for faculty, however, even though the activity itself offers intel-lectual rewards, professional disincentives discourage extended involve-ment, especially for those faculty still in progress through tenure and promotion in rank.

Outreach is also seen in emergent definitions of technology transfer. Technology transfer is activity that is highly interactive and market driven, with extensive and synergistic linkages between university and industry (Fairweather, 1996, p. 8). The line between basic and applied research becomes blurred, but the goal is to understand changing markets, industrial needs, and technological opportunities, using information to modify the direction of future faculty research. In such examples, industry profession-als and university faculty work together on inquiry activities. Where such work is common, universities have removed traditional barriers that pro-hibit faculty engagement and even have found incentives for participation. Fairweather acknowledges the fundamental disagreement between tradi-tional academic norms and faculty behavior, stating that "the pervasive atti-tude in our land-grant universities is that applied work is not important" (1996, p. 9). Yet, he advocates raising knowledge and technology transfer to central status in the area of service (outreach) and enhancing the value of service in personnel decisions. Applied research with demonstrable ben-efit to the region or locality, though not published in traditional outlets, should be rewarded as activity that supports the institutional mission.

The problems solved and knowledge gained from university-industry technology transfer are applicable to other disciplinary configurations and outreach partnership activities. How we encourage faculty to participate in activities that promote the public good rather than private gain (Fairweather, 1996, p. 131) may come down to institutional priorities and systemic support. It requires decreased reliance on quantitative process assessments and increased assessment of impact.

Evaluating Outreach Performance

Those advocating greater recognition for outreach performance recognize the problems surrounding its assessment on many college campuses. It is difficult to document the scholarly quality, rigor, and impact of outreach performance when a publication record is the extent of documentation expected for evaluation of faculty performance (Schon, 1995). Just as new definitions of outreach performance have unfolded, there is also need for new forms of documentation and evaluation that capture the nature and purpose of faculty outreach activity.

Multiple models and strategies exist for evaluating outreach performance (Adam and Roberts, 1993; Diamond, 1999; McMahon and Caret, 1997). The models may be tied to uniform institutional definitions of work or based on disciplinary or departmental descriptors. There are considerable differences in definitions and expectations based on institution type, which is appropriate given diversity in institutional missions. As with teaching and research, institutions need to define their niche for outreach performance, articulate expectations, and design appropriate assessment strategies. Lack of uniformity makes presenting a succinct review of evaluation schemas somewhat problematic here, but I will provide some examples and raise some evaluation issues common in conversations about assessing outreach performance.

General Assessment Criteria. When assessing outreach performance, Votruba (1997) stresses the need for evaluation standards of quality and productivity, regardless of specific criteria used. He emphasizes that outreach work should provide added value and suggests that evaluators examine the extent to which a particular outreach program or service has demonstrable impact, the difference made by the outreach work, and the extent to which it enhances the institution's mission.

In every form of scholarship, there is a "common sequence of unfolding stages" (Glassick, Huber, and Maeroff, 1997, p. 24) that can be explicitly articulated for evaluation purposes. These stages, adapted for outreach, include clear goals, adequate preparation, appropriate methods, significant results (impact), effective presentation (for the beneficiary and the field), and reflective critique. The faculty member should document the outreach project with appropriate materials, addressing each of the emerging stages (Glassick, Huber, and Maeroff), often through the use of a portfolio (Froh, Gray, and Lambert, 1993; Sandmann, 1996). Materials submitted likely vary based on the project, and beneficiaries of outreach activity may also be invited to provide evaluative feedback.

The narrative portion of the portfolio, including reflective critique, is particularly important for assessing outreach performance. Narrative reveals rationales of outreach projects; how they were undertaken; how activities presented support institutional priorities; how they integrate with faculty interests, research, and instruction; and how they have value-added benefits for faculty (Sandmann, 1996). Faculty articulate how knowledge development in their own fields are enhanced in addition to the benefits gained by recipients (Boyer, 1990). They describe the connection between the outreach activity and their academic expertise. This reflection on process and intellectual development is similar to that used in teaching portfolios and differentiates outreach from forms of good citizenship that are typically summarized by a brief listing of activities.

The narrative provides significant information for evaluators to review when considering quality and impact of outreach performance. Again, impact is more important than volume in this evaluation. Honoring outreach activity requires moving away from the technical rationality—seemingly objective measures of dissemination—with which we have historically assessed faculty work, particularly research (Schon, 1995). Citation indexes and counts of publications in prestigious outlets are not appropriate measures for evaluating outreach performance. Instead, evaluation should foster active reflection on the meaning of the outreach activity, as models or prototypes resulting from reflection may be transferred to other settings and new situations (Boyer, 1990; Diamond, 1999; Schon, 1995). Thus, a "culture of evidence" develops that traces the progress of an outreach project. Because the evidence, including the faculty narrative, is not just summative, it can support and honor outreach engagement activity (Ramaley, 2000). Such evaluation will foster outreach work that has greater impact and that is intellectually generative.

The suggestions made by outreach advocates, extensive recording of outreach activity for evaluation purposes, could be viewed as just another burdensome intrusion on faculty time. The value of time spent reflecting about outreach work lies in looking beyond the immediate to the broader institutional climate and context of faculty work. The intent of narrative documentation is not just individual assessment but also to increase dialogue between and among campus units about outreach activity. This approach has potential to foster a campus community where members' different contributions to fulfilling institutional missions are better understood and more fully rewarded. Outreach activities would be public and evaluated by the "highest standards to which scholars can aspire" (Glassick, Huber, and Maeroff, 1997, p. 49).

Efforts to transform assessment of outreach performance are growing. The University of Maryland's Council of University System faculty engaged in this form of campus dialogue and created detailed lists of service and outreach activities from which to develop appropriate documentation and evaluation strategies (McMahon and Caret, 1997). Portland State University adopted the Carnegie/Boyer scholarship classifications (see Chapter Two), including scholarship of application, to support its commitment to service learning activities of faculty and students. Quality, significance, and evaluation criteria are clearly described, allowing disciplinary distinctiveness while making it clear that outreach activity is expected, valued, and rewarded

(Zlotkowski, 1998). On a smaller scale, years after the university president set the symbolic stage for an institutional recommitment to its land-grant mission, Michigan State University's Department of Educational Administration revised its annual evaluation procedure. The revision put outreach scholarly activity on par with traditionally defined research in an effort to recognize the importance of the field-based work in which most of its members were actively involved (Department of Educational Administration, 2000). The department articulated examples and assessment criteria, and many faculty took advantage of the opportunity to share this component of their faculty work in evaluation narratives. There is a special need to define explicit ways of assessing outreach performance in academic units that have external constituents and professional preparation programs, such as the Department of Educational Administration as well as departments of teacher education, health care, public administration, engineering, and social work.

Disciplinary Culture and Outreach Activity. Concern about the locus of evaluation arises when trying to broaden campus dialogue about outreach performance (Edgerton, 1993). Conversation centers on whether individual faculty should be held accountable for meeting the outreach needs of their communities on an institutional, local, regional, state, and global level and whether larger groups of faculty should have collective responsibility for outreach performance rather than individuals. Some argue that societal problems are too complex, external pressures for outreach activity too great, and resources too scarce to rely on the individual entre-preneurial faculty model of years passed (Amey and Brown, 2000; Edgerton, 1993; Sandmann and Flynn, 1997). But moving to collective accountability requires change in institutional policy *and* change in departmental cultures. The latter is perhaps a more significant and difficult challenge and is tied closely to disciplinary cultures.

Because of the influence of disciplinary cultures and values on faculty work, learned societies and their campus counterparts (academic departments and disciplinary subunits) should take on the mission of outreach activity more directly. This involves articulating clearer definitions of what outreach means within disciplines and requires setting new standards of what it means to be a sociologist or an educator or an engineer when that profession includes an outreach role (Adam and Roberts, 1993; Ramaley, 2000; Votruba, 1997). The Center for Instructional Development at the University of Syracuse invited twenty scholarly societies, learned associations, and accrediting agencies to help define scholarly work of faculty in various disciplines, including the scholarship of application (outreach). Each disciplinary group addressed the nature of outreach activity, including evaluation, without being overly prescriptive or institutionally inappropriate. The results included new professional identities that could be enacted and assessed and that could meet the needs of the discipline across the full range of intellectual work. (See Diamond and Adam, 1993, for detailed descriptions of disciplinary outreach definitions.)

Involvement of learned societies and professional associations in discussions about outreach performance and professional identity has other benefits for the future of outreach activity. When outreach is valued and part of the professional conversation among faculty within the disciplines, graduate students and junior faculty learn the importance of outreach from the beginning of their careers. Engaging in outreach activity requires modifying the traditional research preparation that dominates graduate preparation programs. Socializing graduate students and new faculty into the domain of outreach requires finding ways to orient faculty towards constituent cultures, values, and needs. It demands a respect for constituents' knowledge. It requires that faculty understand that one cannot fully determine professional activities and direction without considering constituents' needs and voices. It suggests that faculty should learn how to communicate intellectual knowledge in multiple languages (administrative, client, public, and so on) as well as in the jargon understood by disciplinary colleagues.

Institutionalizing Support for Outreach Performance

Before outreach activity becomes more common, incentive and reward structures need to include resource streams for efforts and standards for evaluating quality and productivity. Institutional leadership should focus institutional and departmental policies and practices around outreach activity and promote reflective evaluation of such activities (Senge, 1990; Votruba, 1997). Administrators (department chairs, deans, directors, and so forth) should be held accountable for incorporating support of outreach activity into unit planning. Thus, while the academic department or college/school may or may not be the unit of analysis in assessing outreach performance, the academic administrator becomes vested in developing a culture of outreach likely to yield more activity.

There is a difference between elevating, intensifying, and ratcheting up an institutional priority such as outreach and linking this priority to the rest of faculty activities (Austin and Moore, 1997). Real change requires rethinking the nature of academic work, redefining mission to include outreach, and integrating attention and commitment across the mission. The last requisite is perhaps the most difficult to accomplish, and it raises the question, How can outreach work flow seamlessly into research and teaching? An answer demands systemic reform rather than piecemeal remedies.

Outreach activities are often left to individual faculty members rather than being part of a collective agenda. Just as instructional development programs are often peripheral to mainstream faculty work and therefore affect only those with a priori investment, encouraging outreach often motivates only those who already are involved. Others may see the work as tangential. As administrators work to improve the quality and acceptance of outreach performance, they need to recognize the complexity of faculty work and account for the potential effects on other areas of work when one piece of the puzzle is changed. A systemic approach accounts for interrelationships of external, institutional, departmental, and individual factors influencing faculty work and priorities, including outreach activity. It challenges traditional hierarchical and linear structures about faculty work activities in which outreach likely ranks very near the bottom.

Strategies to encourage outreach within the traditional hierarchical structures will fail to transform the institution for several reasons. Faculty roles are increasingly complex in all institutions, but responsibilities have been added with little reshaping of the surrounding environment, little reorienting of institutional reward structures, and little examination of the interrelated components of the institutional structure in which the work takes place (Colbeck, 1998). Without incorporating a more systemic approach and understanding, most change efforts are relegated to the individual level—a single faculty member involving herself in a constituent-based knowledge activity. The underlying belief is that academic culture can be transformed from individual gain to common good by the cumulative effects of reforming individual faculty and their beliefs about outreach performance.

The assumption that institutional or departmental transformation results from aggregated changes in individual faculty beliefs and behaviors is unproven. Instead, a more holistic perspective and systemic support system is required, afforded through departments, colleges, and institutions. Seeing connections between components of outreach performance processes and the ways these processes change faculty roles requires a different analytic framework. In the end, outreach activities occur within the confines of organizational structures, policies, and practices because they are conducted by faculty employed under collegiate contracts. Successful outreach innovations can only be institutionalized by critically challenging the current architecture of postsecondary education.

A changed course of direction for the connected college and university of the future depends on transformational change—a break from the traditions of linear change models that have been the norm in academe. A systems approach enables us to understand how various aspects of the environment influence and interact to affect involvement in outreach activity. It also allows us to develop synergistic understandings for how outreach performance might be successfully integrated into the complexities of faculty work.

Faculty participation in outreach addresses societal and constituent needs and helps fulfill institutional mission and values. It also benefits faculty themselves in terms of revitalized teaching, new research opportunities, and overall intellectual vitality (Hirsch and Lynton, 1995). A focus on outreach promotes the scholarship of application through better definitions; integration with teaching, research, and service; and institutionalization of effective evaluation mechanisms. Reconnecting to institutional mission through outreach performance is one of the most important challenges facing colleges and universities in the foreseeable future.

References

Adam, B. E, and Roberts, A. O. "Differences Among Disciplines." In R. M. Diamond and B. E. Adam (eds.), *Recognizing Faculty Work: Rewards Systems for the Year 2000.* New Directions for Higher Education, no. 81. San Francisco: Jossey-Bass, 1993.

Amey, M. J., and Brown, D. F. "Interdisciplinary Collaboration and Academic Work." Paper presented at the Annual Meeting of the Association for the Study of Higher Education, Sacramento, Calif., Nov. 2000.

Austin, A. E., and Moore, K. M. *Realigning Institutional Missions and Faculty Work: A Project on Strategies and Lessons.* East Lansing: Michigan State University, 1997.

Barr, R. B., and Tagg, J. "From Teaching to Learning: A New Paradigm for Undergraduate Education." *Change,* 1995, 27(6), 12–25.

Boyer, E. L. *Scholarship Reconsidered: Priorities of the Professoriate.* Princeton, N.J.: The Carnegie Foundation for the Advancement of Teaching, 1990.

Colbeck, C. L. "Merging in a Seamless Blend: How Faculty Integrate Teaching and Research." *Journal of Higher Education,* 1998, 69(6), 647–671.

Department of Educational Administration. *Faculty Annual Evaluation.* East Lansing: Michigan State University, 2000.

Diamond, R. M. *Aligning Faculty Rewards with Institutional Mission: Statements, Policies, and Guidelines.* Bolton, Mass.: Anker, 1999.

Diamond, R. M., and Adam, B. E. *Recognizing Faculty Work: Rewards Systems for the Year 2000.* New Directions for Higher Education, no. 81. San Francisco: Jossey-Bass, 1993.

Edgerton, R. "The Re-examination of Faculty Priorities." *Change,* 1993, 25(4), 10–26.

Fairweather, J. *Faculty Work and Public Trust: Restoring the Value of Teaching and Public Service in American Academic Life.* Boston: Allyn & Bacon, 1996.

Fear, F. A., and Sandmann, L. R. "Unpacking the Service Category: Reconceptualizing University Outreach for the 21st Century." *Continuing Higher Education Review,* 1997, 59(3), 117–122.

Froh, R. C., Gray, P. J., and Lambert, L. M. "Representing Faculty Work: The Professional Portfolio." In R. M. Diamond and B. E. Adam (eds.), *Recognizing Faculty Work: Rewards Systems for the Year 2000.* New Directions for Higher Education, no. 81. San Francisco: Jossey-Bass, 1993.

Glassick, C. E., Huber, M. T., and Maeroff, G. I. *Scholarship Assessed: Evaluation of the Professoriate.* San Francisco: Jossey Bass, 1997.

Hirsch, D., and Lynton, E. *Bridging Two Worlds: Professional Service and Service Learning.* Boston: New England Resource Center for Higher Education, University of Massachusetts, 1995.

Lynton, E. A. *Making the Case for Professional Service.* Washington, D.C.: American Association for Higher Education, 1995.

McMahon, J. D., and Caret, R. K. "Redesigning the Faculty Roles and Rewards Structure." *Metropolitan University,* 1997, 7(4), 11–22.

Ramaley, J. A. "Embracing Civic Responsibility." *AAHE Bulletin,* 2000, 52(7), 9–13.

Rice, R. E. *Making a Place for the New American Scholar.* Washington, D.C.: American Association of Higher Education, 1996.

Sandmann, L. *Developing a Faculty Outreach Portfolio.* Lansing: Michigan State University, 1996.

Sandmann, L., and Flynn, M. *A Model for Neighborhood Redevelopment Through University-Mediated Intervention: Evaluation Research Plan.* East Lansing: Michigan State University, 1997.

Schon, D. A. "The New Scholarship Requires a New Epistemology: Knowing in Action." *Change,* 1995, 27(6), 26–39.

Senge, P. M. "The Leader's New Work: Building Learning Organizations." *Sloan Management Review,* 1990, 32(1), 7–23.

Votruba, J. C. "Strengthening the University's Alignment with Society's Challenges and Strategies." *Journal of Public Service and Outreach*, 1997, *1*(1), 29–36.
Zlotkowski, E. (ed.). *Successful Service Learning Programs: New Models of Excellence in Higher Education.* Bolton, Mass.: Anker, 1998.

MARILYN J. AMEY *is associate professor of higher education and coordinator of the higher, adult, and lifelong education program at Michigan State University.*

Faculty work frequently involves joint production of teaching and research, teaching and service, or research and service. Evaluation should recognize and encourage integration of faculty work roles.

Integration: Evaluating Faculty Work as a Whole

Carol L. Colbeck

Faculty evaluation serves several important functions, including improving faculty performance and informing decisions about academic personnel, budget, planning, and resource allocation (Miller, 1987, Romney, 1971). Faculty members' work accomplishes the core goals of colleges and universities as outlined by the American Association of University Professors in 1915: (1) to promote inquiry and advance the sum of human knowledge, (2) to develop general instruction to the students, and (3) to develop experts for the various branches of the public service. Faculty work is usually described in terms of the three corresponding roles of research, teaching, and service.

Two problems surface when describing faculty work in terms of these three roles. The first arises when the *processes* of engaging in teaching, research, and service activities are confused with their *products* or with the institutional *goals* to which the activities and products contribute (Romney, 1971). *Teaching* is variously described as the processes of preparation, classroom instruction, grading, and advising; products such as new courses developed or ratings of instructional effectiveness, or as a college or university goal. Similarly, the term *research* may refer to the processes of gathering and analyzing data or securing funding; to publication, grant, or patent products; or to an institutional goal.

The second problem arises when teaching, research, and service are depicted as mutually exclusive. In interviews, faculty comment that they find their work roles blending, and they often find it difficult to categorize their activities as singularly teaching, or research, or service on workload reports (Clark, 1987; Shulman, 1980). According to Centra (1993, p. 2), "teaching, scholarship, and service are overlapping activities for many faculty members . . . . Evaluation of an individual's performance should take this overlap into account and attempt to determine how one activity contributes to another."

Whether their work is evaluated in distinct categories or as an integrated whole may affect the extent to which faculty jointly produce teaching, research, and service. Faculty members' perceptions of how their institutions define and evaluate roles affects how they do their work. In one study, faculty who perceived that teaching evaluations had especially strong influence on their rewards spent more time on teaching than their colleagues. Similarly, faculty who perceived that evaluations of research had the strongest influence on their rewards spent more time than their colleagues on research (Dornbusch, 1979). According to Fairweather (1996, p. 110), "faculty rewards emphasize the discreteness, not the mutuality, of teaching and research." It is likely that the more institutional evaluations and rewards separate faculty activities and products into mutually exclusive categories, the less faculty will enrich their teaching with their research, inform their research with lessons learned from their professional service, or engage in public scholarship that integrates teaching, research, and service.

In this chapter, I discuss how three common ways of evaluating faculty activities and products segregate faculty work roles. I then present research findings that show the ways and the extent to which some faculty integrate their work roles, and I suggest how to evaluate faculty work as an integrated whole. Finally, I discuss the benefits of integrated evaluation for individual faculty and for the departments and institutions where they work.

Three Methods for Evaluating Faculty Work

Three methods are commonly used to document faculty work for evaluation purposes. Workload reports account for the process of faculty work, and annual reports and promotion and tenure portfolios account for the products of faculty work.

Workload surveys ask faculty to estimate how they allocate time to their various work roles. Faculty estimate either the average number of hours per week or the percent total hours per work term that they engage in the teaching, research, and service activities listed on the reporting form. Some time-consuming activities, such as departmental committee work, are not easy to classify as singularly teaching, research, or service, so are underreported on workload surveys (Clark, 1987). Most workload studies define activity categories as mutually exclusive, obscuring the extent to which some faculty activities fulfill more than one institutional goal (Romney, 1971; Yuker, 1984). In interviews, faculty say their work is varied and hard to quantify, so their responses to workload survey questions only reflect general patterns (Clark, 1987). Many faculty believe that their "activities are so multiple, complex, and interdependent that they cannot be atomized to suit the requirements of a workload questionnaire" (Shulman, 1980).

Faculty document the products of their work in annual reports and promotion and tenure dossiers. In *annual reports,* faculty answer questions about their production of teaching, research, and service during the preceding twelve months. Institutions often use this information to determine merit salary increases (Centra, 1993) and to promote faculty growth and development (Braskamp and Ory, 1994). Evidence of teaching productivity might include number of courses and students taught, number of advisees (including graduate students who have completed degrees), summary scores of student ratings of instruction, and brief descriptions of new courses developed. Faculty provide evidence of research productivity with information about manuscripts accepted, in press, or published; grants or awards received; conference papers presented; or performances given. Service may be divided into institutional, professional, and community service categories. Forms typically ask faculty to list the committees on which they served, the clients they assisted, and the projects to which they lent their expertise (Centra, 1993). As with workload reports, annual report forms require faculty to categorize the products of their work as either teaching, or research, or service. Some annual report forms specifically warn faculty against counting products twice by listing them under more than one work role category. Such cautions reinforce perceptions that each faculty activity fulfills one and only one institutional purpose.

Promotion and tenure dossiers are the most comprehensive documentation of faculty work and are typically comprised of three sections: cumulated and synthesized annual reports of teaching, research, and service products; evidence such as course syllabi or article reprints to substantiate the report; and narrative statements describing how the candidate's work products address personal and institutional goals (Braskamp and Ory, 1994). Narrative statements enable faculty members to "tell the story of what they do and how well they do it" (Braskamp and Ory, 1994, p. 109). The self-reflective statements draw evaluators' attention to what the candidates consider their most important accomplishments, their rationale for their work, and the significance of the work for achieving departmental, institutional, disciplinary, or professional goals. Administrators and senior faculty can facilitate their junior colleagues' professional development by encouraging them to draft their narrative statements early, review the statements with senior faculty, and revise the statements as they progress toward promotion (Boice, 1992). Experienced administrators advise institutions to make expectations for promotion clear and encourage faculty candidates to organize reflective narratives in separate sections for teaching, research, and service (Braskamp and Ory, 1994).

Research Evidence of Faculty Work Role Integration

Workload reports, annual reports, and promotion and tenure dossiers segregate faculty work into mutually exclusive roles, but studies have shown these roles frequently overlap in practice. A few studies have noted that faculty sometimes fulfill two goals with the same activity, but for methodological reasons, the researchers did not document when and how the overlap occurred. When conducting a random time sampling of faculty activities in an engineering department, Ritchey (1959) realized that joint activities were a "complicating factor" in his analysis. He found it "apparent that a staff member who attends a meeting off campus may also be developing himself somewhat professionally as well as possibly helping himself prepare for a class the next day" (p. 453). Ritchey resolved the problem by categorizing such activities by what he considered the primary purpose. In a cost study of medical school faculty work, Lee and Kutina (1974) noted that 45 percent of faculty activities were of a joint nature. They resolved the documentation problem by dividing faculty time spent in joint production of two institutional goals equally among the goals.

Two other institutional workload studies asked faculty to cross-reference their activities with institutional goals. A faculty work analysis conducted at the University of California asked faculty to estimate the proportion of time each work activity contributed to any one or more institutional "outputs." Results showed that, on average, faculty work activities contributed to more than one institutional output objective nearly 40 percent of the time (University of California, 1970). The dean of liberal arts at Arizona State University recently implemented a system that asked faculty to report time spent on activities that integrated teaching and research, research and service, and service and teaching, in addition to time spent on activities that exclusively served teaching, research, or service goals. Humanities, social science, and science faculty respondents to a pilot workload survey reported that they integrated teaching and research 18 percent, research and service 8.2 percent, service and teaching 8.6 percent, and all of their roles 14 percent of the time, respectively (Krahenbuhl, 1998).

I documented similar overlaps between faculty work roles when I conducted structured observations of twelve physicists' and English professors' work activities at two universities (Colbeck, 1995, 1998). I observed three faculty members in each discipline at Vantage University, an elite private research university, and at Cosmopolitan State, a public master's level university, for five nonconsecutive days each. The observed faculty were all white, male, full professors in the prime of their careers. On each observation day, I asked the faculty member to report the timing and nature of the work activities he engaged in since the close of the previous work day. The sample included 4,049 discrete work activities that occurred over a total of 1,030 hours. I classified all observed and reported work activities for the academic goals accomplished (teaching, research, or service), the specific action performed, and the amount of time in minutes that each action contributed to one or more academic goal.

By observing faculty actually at work, I documented many periods when faculty engaged in activities that fulfilled more than one goal. An example of teaching and research integration occurred when an English professor read and analyzed a novel for class discussion, knowing that he was scheduled to present a conference paper about the novel's author in two months. A week later, the professor used his class notes when drafting his conference presentation. A physicist integrated teaching and research when he explored the next steps on a research project with undergraduate and graduate student members of his research team over lunch at the student union. One English professor and one physicist I observed integrated professional service and research as they reviewed papers in their specialties for conferences they were hosting. Two English professors fulfilled both teaching and public service goals when they taught community groups. Several faculty blended department administrative work and teaching when they worked with colleagues or administrators to plan departmental course schedules.

The amount of time that all faculty I observed integrated teaching, research, or service is shown in Table 4.1. On average, they engaged in activities that fulfilled teaching goals 62.7 percent of their time. Their activities met solely teaching goals 38.2 percent of the time, met both teaching and research goals 18.8 percent of the time, and met teaching and service goals 5.7 percent of the time. Similarly, the physics and English faculty members engaged in activities that met research goals 42 percent of the time, including activities that met solely research goals (15.7 percent), research and teaching goals (18.8), and research and service goals (7.5 percent). Of the total 20.7 percent of time that met service goals, 7.5 percent also met research goals, 5.7 also met teaching goals, and 7.5 percent met solely service goals. In addition, the twelve faculty also engaged in activities that fulfilled their own personal goals or they engaged in conversation with me an average 4.1 percent and 2.5 percent, respectively, of the total time I observed their work.

Table 4.1.   Percentage of Observed English and Physics Faculty Time Allocated to Singular and Integrated Work Roles.

Activity	English		Physics		
Location	*Cosmopolitan* (353 hours)	*Vantage* (225 hours)	*Cosmopolitan* (259 hours)	*Vantage* (193 hours)	*All*
Teaching only	45.1	44.4	38.0	18.1	38.2
Teaching and Research	19.8	13.5	18.7	22.5	18.8
Research only	6.9	15.9	26.2	17.1	15.7
Research and Service	6.1	3.3	3.6	20.7	7.5
Service only	7.2	7.0	2.9	14.9	7.5
Service and Teaching	8.1	8.0	2.5	2.5	5.7
Personal time only	4.6	4.9	5.0	2.1	4.1
Interview time only	2.2	3.0	3.1	2.1	2.5
Total	100	100	100	100	100

Evaluating the Integration of Faculty Work

Research evidence shows that faculty already integrate their work roles. Failure to account for the ways and the extent to which faculty jointly produce teaching and service, research and teaching, or service and research may underestimate faculty contributions to institutional productivity (Colbeck, 1998). Many faculty, scholars, and administrators believe that such integration improves the quality of their teaching, research, and service products (Bakker, 1995; Clark, 1997; Jenkins, 2000). Systematic and widespread evaluation of faculty work as an integrated whole is needed to determine how much the process of faculty work is actually integrated across all types of institutions and disciplines and to understand the conditions under which such joint production enhances the quality of faculty work products.

Evaluation of faculty work as an integrated whole begins with college or university recognition that linking teaching, research, and service is central to the institution's mission (Jenkins, 2001). Then evaluation information should be gathered that shows how faculty work processes and products are related to institutional goals (Romney, 1971). Workload reports, annual productivity reports, and promotion and tenure portfolios can be modified to reflect and account for the integration of faculty work.

Joint production of teaching, research, and service can be documented in integrated workload reports. Exhibit 4.1 illustrates a form that might be used to cross-reference faculty teaching, research, and service activities

Exhibit 4.1.   Workload Report Form That Cross-References Faculty Activities with all Relevant Institutional Goals.

	Faculty Workload Report	
Activities	Hours/Week	Institutional Goals
Teaching		
Classroom instruction	_____	Percent of time spent on teaching activities that
Preparation	_____	also:
Grading	_____	_____ advanced development of new knowledge/
Individual instruction	_____	arts
Course development	_____	_____ contributed to growth of university,
Meetings/memos	_____	professional, or nonacademic community
Teaching Activity Total	_____	
Research		Percent of time spent on research activities that
Inquiry	_____	also:
Scholarly development	_____	_____ enhanced registered students' development
Logistics/grant work	_____	_____ contributed to growth of university,
Writing/presenting	_____	professional, or nonacademic community
Research Activity Total	_____	
Service		Percent of time spent on service activities that also:
Administrative service	_____	_____ enhanced registered students' development
Professional service	_____	_____ advanced development of new knowledge/
Community service	_____	arts
Service Activity Total	_____	
Total hours/week	_____	

with the institutional goals addressed by those activities. Institutional goals listed include enhancing the development of students registered in the institution, advancing the development of new knowledge and art forms, and contributing to the growth of the institutional, professional, or nonacademic communities (adapted from Romney and Manning, 1974). The form asks faculty to consider the extent to which they integrate activities by estimating, for example, the percent of time they spent on teaching activities that also advanced new knowledge or contributed to the growth of their institutional, professional, or nonacademic communities. To facilitate completion of the form and to encourage ideas for joint production, institutions might attach a list of possible ways to integrate work roles. The list of integrated activities in Table 4.2 is meant to be suggestive rather than exhaustive.

Integrated annual reports provide another way to recognize the extent to which faculty already integrate their work roles and to encourage further integration. Most annual report forms arrange faculty work products according to primary teaching, research, and service goals. An integrated annual report form would also ask faculty to estimate the extent to which a single product contributed to more than one institutional goal. Products listed in the "teaching," "research," and "service" sections of the report would be—as they are now—assumed to contribute 100 percent to the respective institutional goals of enhancing student development, developing new knowledge, and contributing to community growth. Additional short questions would ask for estimates of integration. For each activity listed in the research section, for example, faculty members would estimate the extent to which the activity also enhanced student learning or community growth. Thus, a faculty member might estimate that 50 percent of her

Table 4.2. Suggested Integrated Faculty Work Activities.

Teaching and research	Discuss or present findings from current research in class
	Prepare class related to current research
	Involve students in planning, conduct, analysis, reporting of research
	Conduct research on teaching and learning in one's discipline
Teaching and service	Teach class for community group
	Participate in departmental interdisciplinary curriculum development effort
	Participate in departmental or institutional self-study
	Assist with teaching development activities for new faculty
Research and service	Review manuscripts for academic meetings, journals, or book publishers
	Conduct applied research for community group
	Invited presentations for professional or community groups

effort on an article that she coauthored equally with a student furthered the institutional goal of enhancing student development. Another faculty member who secured external funding for a project to develop and evaluate a new curriculum for first-year students in his discipline might list the grant under research products, but estimate that the grant also contributes 100 percent to the institutional goal of enhancing student development.

While integrated workload and annual reports would encourage faculty to document *how much* their work activities and products meet multiple institutional goals, the narrative statements in their promotion and tenure portfolios could provide opportunities for faculty to explain the rationale for *why* and *how* they integrate teaching, research, and service. Moreover, narrative statements enable faculty to discuss the quality—not just the quantity—of their contributions (Braskamp and Ory, 1994). These statements might be approached in two ways. In the first approach, faculty would write separate short statements about their teaching, research, and service. To demonstrate that their work involves some degree of joint production, however, each section would include information about how this one element of their work has an impact on other institutional goals (Bakker, 1995). Teaching statements, for example, would include information about the scholarly and community impact of the faculty member's pedagogical work. Research statements would include pedagogical and community impact information, and service statements would include pedagogical and scholarly impact information. A potential liability of this approach would be duplication of information across the three statements.

The second approach to promotion and tenure narratives would ask faculty to describe their contributions to institutional goals in a single integrated statement. Braskamp and Ory suggest that faculty candidates "make a case by integrating the various forms of work and indicating how each reinforces the other" (1994, p. 112) and that candidates should use evidence to support their assertions of quality. Braskamp and Ory have found that faculty seldom write integrated reports, so they "need assistance and mentoring to accomplish this" (1994, p. 112). Faculty efforts should also be supported by departmental and institutional policies that provide explicit criteria for evaluating and rewarding the links between faculty work roles (Jenkins, 2001).

Benefits of Evaluating Faculty Work as an Integrated Whole

Evaluating and rewarding faculty work as an integrated whole will help faculty and the colleges and universities where faculty work. Faculty attend to the ways they are evaluated and adjust their direction and level of effort accordingly (Dornbusch, 1979). Faculty also judge their institutions, at least in part, by whether evaluations enhance or constrain their professional opportunities. An integrated approach to evaluating their work would widen faculty members' broadly defined scholarly opportunities (Glassick,

Huber, and Maeroff, 1997). Faculty perceptions of meaningful rewards for both teaching and research have led to positive correlations between their teaching and research productivity (Boice, 1984).

A system of evaluation and rewards that recognizes the entire scope of faculty work also recognizes that faculty are complex, professional workers (Scott, 1998). According to organizational theorist W. Richard Scott, organizations can respond to increasing technical complexity by subdividing work, thereby increasing organizational complexity and managerial responsibility. Alternatively, organizations can hire professionals—highly qualified, flexible, and complex workers who handle unpredictable work problems independently. The current academic evaluation and reward system fragments faculty members' work roles and may contribute to increasing subdivision and deprofessionalization of faculty work.

Evaluating faculty work as an integrated whole provides several benefits to colleges and universities. Documentation of the current extent of joint production would provide a more accurate picture of individual, departmental, and institutional productivity. Moreover, such documentation would allow institutions to gain a comprehensive view of how faculty time and activities contribute to various institutional goals and inform resource allocation decisions and would suggest how some activities might be adjusted to improve the achievement of institutional goals (Romney, 1971). As faculty respond to requests to document how their activities and products contribute to multiple institutional goals, they are likely to find more creative ways to bring their research into the classroom, involve students in cutting-edge research, apply their research to community problems, and teach and learn from community members. A climate that encourages integration of teaching, research, and service is fundamental to the soundness of universities, and it provides for the best use of faculty resources, the effectiveness of the profession, and full benefits to students and other beneficiaries of college and university work (Krahenbuhl, 1998).

References

Bakker, G. "Using 'Pedagogical-Impact Statements' to Make Teaching and Research Symbiotic Activities." *Chronicle of Higher Education,* Mar. 17, 1995, p. B3.

Boice, R. "Reexamination of Traditional Emphases in Traditional Faculty Development." *Research in Higher Education,* 1984, *21*, 195–209.

Boice, R. *The New Faculty Member: Supporting and Fostering Professional Development.* San Francisco: Jossey-Bass, 1992.

Braskamp, L. A., and Ory, J. C. *Assessing Faculty Work: Enhancing Individual and Institutional Performance.* San Francisco: Jossey-Bass, 1994.

Centra, J. A. *Reflective Faculty Evaluation: Enhancing Teaching and Determining Faculty Effectiveness.* San Francisco: Jossey-Bass, 1993.

Clark, B. R. *The Academic Life: Small Worlds, Different Worlds.* Princeton, N.J.: The Carnegie Foundation for the Advancement of Teaching, 1987.

Clark, B. R. "The Modern Integration of Research Activities with Teaching and Learning." *Journal of Higher Education,* 1997, *68*, 241–255.

Colbeck, C. L. "Weaving Seamless Lives: Organizational and Disciplinary Influences on the Integration and Congruence of Faculty Work." Unpublished doctoral dissertation, School of Education, Stanford University, 1995.

Colbeck, C. L. "Merging in a Seamless Blend: How Faculty Integrate Teaching and Research." *Journal of Higher Education,* 1998, *69*(6), 647–671.

Dornbusch, S. M. "Perspectives from Sociology: Organizational Evaluation of Faculty Performances." In D. R. Lewis and W. E. Becker Jr. (eds.), *Academic Rewards in Higher Education.* Cambridge, Mass.: Ballinger, 1979.

Fairweather, J. S. *Faculty Work and Public Trust: Restoring the Value of Teaching and Public Service in American Academic Life.* Boston: Allyn & Bacon, 1996.

Glassick, C. E., Huber, M. T., and Maeroff, G. I. *Scholarship Assessed: Evaluation of the Professoriate.* San Francisco: Jossey-Bass, 1997.

Jenkins, A. "The Relationship Between Teaching and Research: Where Does Geography State and Deliver?" *Journal of Geography in Higher Education,* 2000, *24*(3), 325–351.

Jenkins, A. "How (or Whether?) to Integrate Research into Classroom Teaching for All Students and All Higher Education Institutions." Paper presented at the Schreyer National Conference, University Park, Penn., Mar. 30, 2001.

Krahenbuhl, G. S. "Faculty Work: Integrating Responsibilities and Institutional Needs." *Change,* 1998, *30*(6), 18–25.

Lee, M., and Kutina, K. L. "Sampling and Measurement Error in Faculty Activity and Effort Reporting." *Journal of Medical Education,* 1974, *49*, 989–991.

Miller, R. I. *Evaluating Faculty for Promotion and Tenure.* San Francisco: Jossey-Bass, 1987.

Ritchey, J. A. "An Unusual Work Sampling Application." *Journal of Industrial Engineering,* 1959, *10*(6), 450–455.

Romney, L. C. *Faculty Activity Analysis: Overview and Major Issues.* Technical Report, no. 24. Boulder, Colo.: National Center for Higher Education Management Systems, 1971.

Romney, L. C., and Manning, C. W. *Faculty Activity Analysis: Interpretation and Uses of Data.* Technical Report, no. 54. Boulder, Colo.: National Center for Higher Education Management Systems, 1974.

Scott, W. R. *Organizations: Rational, Natural, and Open Systems.* (4th ed.) Englewood Cliffs, N.J.: Prentice Hall, 1998.

Shulman, C. H. "Do Faculty Really Work That Hard?" *ASHE-ERIC Higher Education Currents,* Oct. 1980, 5–6, 11–12.

University of California. *Faculty Effort and Output Study.* Berkeley, Calif.: Office of the President, University of California, 1970.

Yuker, H. E. *Faculty Workload: Research, Theory, and Interpretation.* ASHE-ERIC Higher Education Research Report, no. 10. Washington D.C.: Association for the Study of Higher Education, 1984.

CAROL L. COLBECK is associate professor of higher education and a senior research associate in the Center for the Study of Higher Education, Pennsylvania State University. She conducts research on faculty integration of teaching, research, and service, and relationships between organizational climate, faculty teaching, and student learning.

5

A volatile mix—new technologies and academic identities.

The Impact of Technology on Faculty Performance and Its Evaluation

Craig McInnis

Universities worldwide are in the early stages of an unprecedented period of rapid and complex change, driven, to a substantial degree, by the introduction and proliferation of new information technologies. The conjunction of the globalization of higher education, the intense market competition that comes with new frontiers and opportunities, and fundamental shifts in the expectations society has of higher education is transforming universities and challenging the capacity of faculty to work effectively and productively. New technologies are a key ingredient in this transformation process, and their influence on academic work is increasingly pervasive, reaching far beyond the everyday adjustments to new ways of performing core tasks.

Technology is changing the way faculty work is defined and evaluated. Data sources now have the potential to provide comprehensive and detailed information about the quality and quantity of faculty and student work. It is possible to monitor and verify the performance of both individuals and institutions from diverse sources. The new technologies are also changing the criteria by which faculty performance is judged in two important respects: the extent to which faculty actually use technologies in their diverse tasks and the effective use of technologies in improving student learning outcomes.

The impact of new technologies on faculty work cannot be considered in isolation from the broader external forces driving the transformation of universities. It is also important to place the impact of new technologies on the performance and evaluation of faculty work in the context of other major trends redefining the nature of faculty work and the overall standing of the profession, including the changing expectations and needs of students, the growing diversity of the student population, the broadening of modes of delivery and forms of learning, and demands for more rigorous system and institutional approaches to quality assurance.

Clark (2000, p. 12) points to the growth of demand overload and "turbulent environments" created by four converging trends common to many higher education systems around the world: the growth in the number and type of students (including external, mixed mode, and part-time), the demand for occupationally specific skills and generic skills relevant to employment, the expectation that universities will directly and immediately contribute to economic and technological progress, and knowledge growth ("the most troubling trend of all") across all fields. This last factor is most relevant to the discussion of the impact of technology on faculty work. The individual, everyday management of knowledge—its creation, preservation, synthesis, and transmission—is at the core of the academic endeavor. Indeed, it is this that defines the profession. Until now this has given faculty a special, though not exclusive, role in society. However, a report on Australia's information future highlighted two key influences on the academic environment relevant to all developed countries at this time: "In the knowledge economy, the Academies and university researchers are losing their monopoly in knowledge production. Increasingly, the Academies and universities are becoming knowledge receivers and transformers of knowledge as well as generators of knowledge" (Gallagher, 1999, p. ix).

Not that this mix of roles is new to faculty, but the arrival of new providers of higher education has focused attention on the differences between them and conventional institutions. With the loss of monopoly in knowledge production and generation, it is inevitable that other constituencies will have a stronger say in what is valued about faculty work and how the work is evaluated.

Impact of New Technologies on Performance of Academic Work

The ideals of academic work contrast with the central features of for-profit technology-based providers (Cunningham and others, 2000). Collegiality, autonomy, academic freedom, the belief that teaching and research are—and ought to be—linked, and academic control over most aspects of the educational process are under threat from new providers. In contrast, the new providers focus on specific target client groups and a relatively limited range of courses, ability and willingness to design courses to suit clients, and widespread use of professional practitioners instead of academics to teach professionally relevant courses. Not surprisingly, the for-profit providers take a strong interest in the evaluation of all aspects of the education process.

Involvement of for-profit providers is influenced by growing demand for standardized products, services, and technical infrastructure and by sophisticated communication systems in the globalized economy. This press for standardization in product and delivery has considerable implications for the evaluation of faculty work, even for faculty not employed by for-profit providers. The Cunningham study identifies the "potential for communication and information technologies to reduce the fixed costs of education" and "dissatisfaction by industry with the responsiveness of traditional providers" as factors demanding change in the way faculty generally conceive of their work. "In the for-profit organizations, disaggregation of the academic roles of curriculum developer, teacher, researcher, examiner and community service provider is proceeding apace, and even in the traditional higher education sector there is movement in this direction" (Cunningham and others, 2000, p. xiii). More specifically, Coaldrake and Stedman (1999, p. 7) suggest the following tasks normally undertaken by faculty that could be readily assumed by others in a technologically driven environment:

- assessing students' credentials and giving credit for entry;
- designing and coordinating units and courses of study;
- designing and developing resources used in learning, including textbooks, videos, and computer packages;
- assessing resources for quality;
- navigating and advising students through choices of study options;
- delivering instruction—for example, by lecturing or demonstrating practical work in laboratories;
- acting as guide and mentor to students, either individually or in groups;
- assessing, evaluating and providing feedback on student progress; and,
- certifying completion of award programs.

This "unbundling" of academic work and its redistribution outside teaching is already occurring to varying degrees in conventional university environments. The use of new technologies has added to the increasing influence of professional administrators and technical specialists over academic work as boundaries dissolve and collaboration becomes the prerequisite for success. Application of technologies is blurring the roles of creators, providers, and distributors of knowledge. Activities of technology specialists now impinge on the core activities of teaching and research (McInnis, 1998). The loss of academic control, and therefore identity, over technology-dependent work is a source of tension and frustration. Moreover, the technologies give a new edge to the arguments that academics are working with dated assumptions about the holistic nature of their work: "The ultimate tenet about faculty work, which is influenced by beliefs about the importance of intrinsic motivation and the overlap of teaching and research, is that faculty members can be productive in all aspects of faculty work" (Fairweather, 1999, p. 59). New technologies, in the mix with for-profit opportunities, confront the deeply embedded belief that faculty can and ought to be productive on all fronts.

Impact of Technologies on Teaching

Faculty are typically more concerned with the impact of technologies on their teaching than on their research. In a recent Australian study (McInnis, 2000), faculty were asked to indicate which activities have had the most impact on changes in their working hours in the last five years. Two-thirds reported that developing course materials for new technologies had a major impact on their changing work hours. Designing and scanning in on-line materials had a marked impact on 43 percent of faculty. Administrative work is also increasing because of the design and implementation of new technologies, especially concerning teaching.

A common observation about the impact of technology on teaching is that faculty can expect to shift their energies from "the transmission of information towards the management and facilitation of student learning" (Coaldrake and Stedman, 1999, p. 7). For many faculty, "transmitting information" is an inaccurate description of what they do when they teach. Personal engagement with the knowledge is what gives the most inspiring teachers their identity as academics rather than being mere "facilitators." Conveying that sense of engagement to students is properly considered the mark of a good teacher.

The use of on-line teaching and learning systems provides faculty with opportunities for change in three areas in particular: organizing student groups, instructing students and supporting student learning, and evaluating student performance. The organization of student groups provides potentially more efficient management of routine administrative tasks and basic record keeping. On-line systems also provide a valuable tool for creating and managing learning communities, especially where students are required to work collaboratively. Although the nature, extent, and value of student involvement in discussion forums is still unclear, it is generally the case that many of the innovations in teaching with new technologies emphasize faculty opportunity to structure and monitor interactions between students. It is also now apparent that the amount of time and energy required of faculty to achieve this potential is quite substantial.

The impact of technologies on instruction can be considered on a number of levels. On one level, faculty use new technologies to enhance their preferred style of teaching. They can present lectures with technical sophistication using computer-managed electronic presentations, make notes available on a Web site for students to download and store, and communicate with students by e-mail. These are not trivial advances in quality of presentation, efficiency of dissemination, and the opportunity for students to interact with their teachers.

The enhancement of teaching precipitated by technologies does not, however, necessarily lead to a deeper level of change in the performance of academic work, that is, the shift to a more reflective approach to teaching as scholarship. Such a shift does not require technologies, but the demand of technologies has forced a growing number of faculty to question fundamental assumptions about the way in which teaching and learning is conducted: "Faculty who begin experimenting with information technology in education often undergo 'conversion experiences' that leave them better teachers. Their effort to understand what is different about teaching with technology versus teaching without it forces them to reflect more consciously on the teaching and learning processes, and often leads them into discussions with colleagues—and perhaps students—about the relative merits of various teaching approaches" (Gilbert, 1996, p. 22).

Demands for more diagnostic feedback on academic progress from students as well as from those responsible for quality assurance and funding will doubtless increase. Most academics believe that providing students with information that enables them to improve their performance is a desirable goal. This is extremely difficult with large groups, but teaching technologies are providing a partial answer. The use of on-line systems for evaluating student performance has an obvious appeal where large classes are involved. Distance education strategies have been used in campus-based universities in Australia and elsewhere for some time to alleviate some of the demands of teaching large groups as well as to meet the needs of the 50 percent or so of mature-age students who are enrolled part-time. Courses of study will increasingly provide for on-line assessment in the form of multiple-choice questions and rapid, diagnostic feedback on tutorial or laboratory tasks.

One of the most publicized consequences of new technologies in higher education has been the growth in electronic plagiarism—a particularly salient example of the way in which faculty work is being reshaped. Not only does electronic plagiarism mean more work, it adds another layer of accountability for faculty. Available electronic detection tools aimed at minimizing plagiarism require more administration to make monitoring effective. Faculty have to devise creative new forms of assessment to counter the problem, provide guidelines for students on the ethical issues involved, and possibly conduct random checks on the originality of student work in addition to the normal processes of grading. The ultimate responsibility for managing the more complex assessment processes will fall to faculty, and their performance will be evaluated accordingly.

New Demands for Group Solutions

Universities are forming alliances to make new technologies affordable in the face of competition from large-scale global commercial providers with access to mass knowledge production and distribution networks. Universities now rely considerably on their control over accreditation and their reputations for rigor in quality assurance to sustain their market position (Levin, 2000). They are attempting to form consortia with other universities and corporations, partly to remain viable within their own traditions, but also to head off real or imagined global competition. The threat to institutional viability comes simultaneously from within higher education systems. Public universities in most countries have experienced a major decline in the proportion of income they receive from government over the last decade, and their survival is dependent on their ability to reduce costs and to generate income. The search for efficiency means that universities are being selective in the teaching and research they do and in the forms of delivery they use. These developments are taking place against a backdrop of a growing number of alternative and highly commercial higher education providers, which are also responding to the conditions that make the uses of technologies crucial to the changing nature of academic work.

New technologies require faculty to share their work with others, partly because of the need for technical expertise and partly because the scale of the teaching enterprise in emerging consortia requires systematic planning and sophisticated delivery beyond the capacity of individual faculty. Because technologies are being used to accommodate larger numbers of students and to capture bigger markets, major changes to the way in which work is organized are involved. For example, the development of multimedia materials and interactive on-line courses require substantial investments of time and frequently require the capacity to work in teams. According to Fairweather (1999, p. 93), "For most departments, the key to increasing teaching and research productivity may lie in looking for group solutions rather than in relying on each faculty member simultaneously to increase productivity levels in teaching and research."

Of course, teams involve a range of specialists. Faculty may have to yield to the advice of technical specialists on matters that they previously would have decided without consulting others. The primary job of faculty is to make sense of the massive and growing knowledge in their fields, so the knowledge can be organized and delivered by technical experts who will exert considerable influence over the timing and delivery and assessment of student work (Armstrong, 2000). Whether faculty will be formally appraised on the basis of their ability to work with teams, rewards for teaching and research are more likely to flow to those who can most effectively use the skills of academic and technical specialists. In Australia, for example, the expectation that faculty will collaborate on teaching, research, and commercial ventures, both within and outside the institution, has become the norm. Indeed, it is considerably less common for academics to attract major competitive grants working alone.

Impact of New Technologies on Evaluation of Faculty

Faculty are already citing usage rates and reach of their electronic delivery modes in support of applications for appointment and promotion. The time, location, and nature of student activity can be readily accessed and analyzed. Faculty will increasingly use whatever data they can gather from electronic records on student learning outcomes to add to their credibility. Of course, this is a two-edged sword. If an instructor can monitor student progress and outcomes, so, too, can supervisors and quality auditors. The latter are likely to have a particular interest in the measurement of student learning outcomes and performance over time and relative to other teachers—not only within a particular institution but across national and international systems.

Technology enables greater supervision of academic work and opens the potential for systematic control over quality and output of work, from gathering and storage of student feedback on teaching to monitoring of student progress. Technology can be applied to the evaluation of faculty in several ways. Although students' on-line evaluation of teaching is basically just a more efficient way of doing business, it allows for more regular and unsolicited feedback to be encouraged and monitored by supervisors. New technologies are suggesting new ways to measure performance that had not been considered previously. It is now possible to monitor Web-site use, level of student participation, availability of faculty, and the timeliness of faculty responses to students.

Although it is hard to imagine that faculty could be faced with detailed analyses like those currently used to monitor the performance of other workers operating in on-line environments, the possibilities present a challenge. With the globalization of on-line learning, growth of expertise in course, student, and faculty evaluation will pose serious issues for faculty. The same is likely to occur with respect to research performance. In Australia, for example, research productivity measured for the purposes of funding universities now requires a close audit of grants and publications. This is done electronically. As research grant applications, progress reports, and publications are increasingly delivered on-line, the capacity of the growing number of stakeholders to maintain records of performance increases.

For many faculty, e-mail has had the most pervasive impact on their teaching and research. As students increasingly expect the university to fit with their lives rather than expecting to accommodate themselves to institutional time frames, their assumptions about faculty availability for consultation and comment on their work have changed. Full-time undergraduates are spending more time on paid work and are accelerating the demand for on-line course materials and for prompt faculty responses via e-mail (McInnis, James, and Hartley, 2000). E-mail generates expectations that ready access means instant response. Although not yet well researched, this phenomenon may contribute to the fragmentation of faculty time. Evaluation of "response time" becomes likely, but at the risk of trivializing faculty work.

Conclusion

Less than a decade ago, Braskamp and Ory said, "a broad repertoire of assessment methods is needed to capture the work of the faculty" (1994, p. 22). A less holistic approach to monitoring academic work may emerge simply because the rationale for maintaining multifaceted faculty roles is getting harder to sustain. For example, the proliferation of support programs for on-line learning skills should reduce the time that faculty spend teaching students basic academic skills. However, these programs have the potential to sharpen the divide between faculty and professional technical and support staff. In the process, expectations for faculty performance may narrow and evaluation of faculty roles may become more compartmentalized.

Pressure to innovate is no longer confined to a minority of early adopters and enthusiasts. The bulk of mainstream faculty are now engaged in revising their approaches, although many are doing so with minimal levels of professional development provided by their universities. Most learn as they go. As more technology-driven evaluation tools emerge, there is likely to be greater pressure for formal certification of performance capability and mandatory professional development. However, this will come at a cost. Release time for learning about new technologies can be a distraction from other scholarly work and deadlines, especially at research-intensive universities (Garrison and Anderson, 2000).

A key difference between conventional and Open and Distance Learning (ODL) institutions is the degree of risk-taking and experimentation possible in the design and implementation of new courses (Devine, 2000). Given the scale and cost of their operations, the ODL institutions must be able to assure prospective students that the courses they take and that the technologies they are required to use are complete, reliable, and robust. Such courses are not easily or quickly changed. In contrast, the physical presence of staff and students on campus enables more flexible adjustments to conventional course design and delivery.

In the early phases of institutional change, faculty are being rewarded for innovations using new technologies in their work, especially for teaching. However, as conventional universities globalize and commercialize their products through new technologies, it is possible that faculty will be evaluated on the extent to which their contributions meet risk-avoidance and reliability criteria. This raises the possibility of constraints on innovation embedded in the evaluation process and managed by experts in the monitoring of performance. The worst-case scenario is that the measures of performance most likely to be used are those that are most accurately measured by and accessible through new technologies. A more positive outlook suggests that faculty will turn the potential of the technologies and the evaluative process to measuring the activities that count most rather than those that can be counted.

References

Armstrong, L. "Distance Learning: An Academic Leader's Perspective on a Disruptive Product." *Change,* 2000, *32*(6), 20–27.
Braskamp, L. A., and Ory, J. C. *Assessing Faculty Work.* San Francisco: Jossey-Bass, 1994.

Clark, B. R. "Collegial Entrepreneurialism in Proactive Universities." *Change,* 2000, *32*(1), 10–19.

Coaldrake, P., and Stedman, L. *Academic Work in the Twenty-First Century.* Occasional Paper Series, Higher Education Division, DETYA, no. 99H. Canberra: Australian Government Publishing Service, 1999.

Cunningham, S., and others. *The Business of Borderless Education.* Evaluations and Investigations Programme, Higher Education Division, DETYA. Canberra: Australian Government Publishing Service, 2000.

Devine, J. "Evaluation and Comparison of Institutional Strategies: New Technologies for Teaching and Learning." Paper presented at the Annual Conference of the European Association for Institutional Research, Berlin, Sept 2000.

Fairweather, J. "The Highly Productive Faculty Member." In W. Tierney (ed.), *Faculty Productivity: Facts, Fictions, and Issues.* New York: Falmer Press, 1999.

Gallagher, M. *Australia's Information Future.* Evaluations and Investigations Programme, Higher Education Division, DETYA. Canberra: Australian Government Publishing Service, 1999.

Garrison, R., and Anderson, T. "Transforming and Enhancing University Teaching: Stronger and Weaker Technological Influences." In T. Evans and D. Nation (eds.), *Changing University Teaching: Reflection on Creating Educational Technologies.* London: Kogan Page, 2000.

Gilbert, S. "Making the Most of a Slow Revolution." *Change,* 1996, *28*(2), 10–23.

Levin, A. "Higher Education at a Crossroads." Earl V. Pullias Lecture in Higher Education. Centre for Higher Education Policy Analysis, Rossier School of Education, University of Southern California, Los Angeles, 2000.

McInnis, C. "Academics and Professional Administrators in Australian Universities: Dissolving Boundaries and New Tensions." *Journal of Higher Education Policy and Management,* 1998, *20*(2), 161–173.

McInnis, C. "Towards New Balance or New Divides? The Changing Work Roles of Academics in Australia." In Malcolm Tight (ed.), *International Perspectives on Higher Education Research.* Vol. 1. New York: Elsevier Science, 2000.

McInnis, C., James, R., and Hartley, R. *Trends in the First Year Experience.* Canberra: Australian Government Publishing Service, 2000.

CRAIG MCINNIS *is professor and director of the Centre for the Study of Higher Education at the University of Melbourne, Australia. He has published widely on changing academic work roles, and is currently conducting a range of research programs concerned with the impact of flexible learning environments on student engagement.*

A systems theory of evaluation provides a framework and critical indicators for evaluating effectiveness of Web-mediated faculty work in creating and transferring knowledge.

A Systems Framework for Evaluation of Faculty Web-Work

Robert J. Marine

Student, institutional, and faculty involvement in distance higher education is growing. Enrollments for academic credit grew between 1995 and 1999 from 700 institutions and 753,640 students to 1,680 institutions and 1,600,000 students. (National Center for Education Statistics, 1999) A recent State Higher Education Executive Officers (SHEEO) survey found that "faculty use of instructional technology" ranked as the top priority among faculty issues, with a mean ranking of 4.02 out of 5, well ahead of second place "attracting and retaining faculty in state" at 3.88 (Russell, 2000). Similarly, the two most important issues for strategic success identified by 464 institutional respondents to a 2001 EDUCAUSE Current Issues survey were funding information technology (IT) and faculty development (Roche, 2000). The number of faculty engaged in Web-mediated teaching, research, and service remains unclear, though the National Center for Education Statistics reported that 5.9 percent of all postsecondary faculty participated in distance education, teaching an average 1.5 such classes, and 52.4 percent of them were for academic credit (National Center for Education Statistics, 2002). This latest available data leaves us with an incomplete picture of the extent and nature of faculty involvement in Web-work.

Sound evaluation of all faculty work should include the specifics of each faculty member's institutional relationships with regard to teaching, research, and community service appointments and should consider academic freedom, selection of materials, technical requirements, and proprietary rights and responsibilities (American Association of University

Professors, 1999). These considerations allow for disparate approaches to evaluating faculty work, whether traditional or mediated by the Web. An integrated systems framework for evaluating Web-work starts with work contexts, specific components of work processes, and goals that faculty are achieving with their work.

Systems Evaluation Model for Faculty Web-Work

When developing and overseeing distance, Internet, and Web-mediated higher and professional continuing education curricula, I also developed a process-integrated system of evaluation for courses and curricula based on general systems theory (Smullyan, 1961; Ford and Lerner, 1992). Recently, I used the model to examine effectiveness of Web-mediated instruction at two universities. The evaluation research demonstrated several differences between traditional and Web-mediated faculty work.

Using traditional approaches, faculty act largely on their own to design, develop, and deliver discipline-based course content, often based on their interests and knowledge production (Green, 1998). The methods of design, development, and delivery for Web-mediated teaching and research require faculty to either become experts in computer technology hardware and software or engage in group processes with technology specialists in six distinct functions: design, curricular and course Web-site development, course delivery and management, student support, and academic database management. Further complications arise when IT availability, support, and strategies vary between administration and instruction or among academic units.

Lack of standardization of resources and processes for Web-work makes meaningful evaluation seem impossible. Most agencies and institutions report only rudimentary quantitative outcomes: number of enrollments by course, number of courses, student grades, and number of research projects. These gross measures give little hint of resources used, and they do not identify specific outcomes, such as gains in students' demonstrated skills or their ability to use new knowledge to modify or enhance decision making.

My systems evaluation model addresses these problems by identifying specific sets of resources used to produce related outcomes. In its general form, the model includes three parallel, articulated systems: faculty, students/constituents, and administration. The faculty system model, depicted in Figure 6.1 includes inputs, processes, and outcomes.

Inputs

Faculty inputs involve characteristics that may affect attitudes about Web-work, the Web-work decision, and how to do Web-work. Existing sources of input data may reside in published departmental and institutional policies

Figure 6.1. Systems Evaluation of Faculty Web-Work.

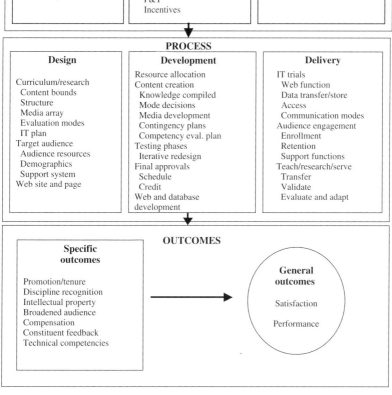

INPUTS		
Perspective of Web-work: Age Gender Ethnicity Rank Security in job Values of discipline Community	**Web-work decision** Personal goals Work styles Perceived proj. value Disciplinary Politics/seniority Department goals Institutional goals Evaluation P&T Incentives	**Mode of Web-work** Technology comfort Social style Career path Opportunity costs Resources Institution culture

PROCESS		

Design
 	
Curriculum/research
Content bounds
Structure
Media array
Evaluation modes
IT plan
Target audience
Audience resources
Demographics
Support system
Web site and page
	Development
	
	Resource allocation
	Content creation
	  Knowledge compiled
	  Mode decisions
	  Media development
	  Contingency plans
	  Competency eval. plan
	Testing phases
	  Iterative redesign
	Final approvals
	  Schedule
	  Credit
	Web and database development
		Delivery
		
		IT trials
		  Web function
		  Data transfer/store
		  Access
		  Communication modes
		  Audience engagement
		  Enrollment
		  Retention
		  Support functions
		  Teach/research/serve
		  Transfer
		  Validate
		  Evaluate and adapt

OUTCOMES

Specific outcomes

Promotion/tenure
Discipline recognition
Intellectual property
Broadened audience
Compensation
Constituent feedback
Technical competencies

General outcomes

Satisfaction

Performance

and official statements of mission and goals, organizational charts, unit function descriptions, faculty curriculum vitae, course catalogues and schedules, and departmental files. Additional perceptual data could be collected from surveys or interviews.

Attitudes about Web-work may be affected by demographic variables, academic rank, discipline participation, position among colleagues in program or department, and geographic location. Age, gender, and ethnicity all have been associated with variation in technology use and attitudes. Discipline and department differences in support for learning and using technology may also influence variation in faculty attitudes. Rank and position in the department may influence perceptions of risk related to Web-work.

Similarly, faculty decisions about whether to do Web-work may be affected by personal goals for teaching, research, and service; faculty styles of instruction or research; judgments of the value of the project; perceptions of institutional values and systems for faculty evaluation; alignment of departmental and institutional goals and mission; and the relative position of the discipline in the institution.

Choices about how to do Web-work are likely to be influenced by faculty comfort with various technologies; social (interpersonal and group interaction) style; perceived career path (traditional academic, entrepreneurial, or administrative); perceptions of the opportunity costs of participating in this endeavor rather than other alternatives; and perceptions of availability and applicability of the institutions' resources for a specific project.

Processes

Three critical Web-work processes are design, development, and delivery. Although they are similar to the analogous processes of traditional faculty work, elements in each make Web-work distinct from traditional faculty work.

Design. The design provides an overarching conceptual framework for the Web-mediated project. Design involves the creation of a Web presence that includes the order and juxtaposition of graphic and content elements (number and order of lessons, modules, assignments, tests, and so forth) that provide the interface with the constituent (student or research consumer) and navigation, or flow, of the user processes. Order of and connections between elements, lessons, or resources are specified through specific hardware or software linkages. The importance of specific types of technology used in defining elements of faculty processes must be delineated in an integrated systems evaluation process. It makes a difference if Blackboard is used as the environment rather than WebCT, for example, because each requires the faculty member and any instructional design team member to create different functional lesson components and different types of linkages between components. Differing resources may be required to use different hardware and software combinations or different platforms.

Design has traditionally been solely the domain of individual faculty. Individuals might consult instructional or research design literature or talk with colleagues who have taught similar courses or done similar research, but the fundamental tools and ideas about design were solely the faculty member's. Not so for the vast majority of faculty members engaged in Web-work. Although the design process may include only the individual faculty preparing a new course or research, design often involves teams in which the faculty member is the content expert but others decide how the content should be presented or made functional. This issue raises questions about intellectual property rights, which are less problematic in traditional instruction or in research projects. Furthermore, many institutions require a uniform Web presence, or design, for every Web-mediated course or research project. This approach requires the faculty member to conform course or project content to fit into the proscribed design and to work with institutionally designated collaborators and hardware and software resources to achieve the design.

Data about the elements of the design process include demographics and assessment of technology use of the constituent population (often by a marketing group and the faculty member); expertise of specific personnel assigned to the project, their capabilities, and limitations on their participation; project budget; type of curricular or research content; the number and different types of modules; planned modes and protocols for evaluation of learning or research efforts; and constituent (end user) resources for engagement. Data for these design elements reside in the project plan at the department or faculty level; in information technology; in instructional systems and marketing support units; and in any prior research or instructional files. This last source might include, for example, student scores on assignments and tests, the types of assignments and tests, and student status or year in program. These data provide information about what the designers considered relevant in creating the Web-project framework. The evaluator can then trace the ways the project implements the framework by analyzing data about each function created during the development phase.

Development. Development is the creation of content materials and functional processes specific to design elements for the transmission of specific ideas, materials, and tools. For a great many faculty, this process is significantly different for Web-work than for traditional academic work. The nature of the Web as a medium for communication and as a technology interface requires layers of technical expertise far beyond the pedagogical and content expertise generally used to do face-to-face instruction, text-based independent learning modules, research tasks, or community service projects.

A growing number of faculty members are learning all of the necessary software programming, application programming, and hardware use and installation required to accomplish their own Web-project development. (Eaton, 2001; Green, 1998, 2001) Most, however, continue to rely on expertise of instructional developers and hardware technicians for coursework and on software programmers and application developers for information systems for research and community service interactions. Whether the faculty member works alone or with one or more technical assistants, Web-work means additional tasks and types of work. Evaluators should collect information about time, personnel, finances (including in-kind interunit transfers), equipment, supplies, and facilities used in the development process.

After data on applied resources is gathered, analysis should connect the use of resources, as directly as possible, to the design elements they enable and the delivery components used to convey them.

Delivery. How faculty members transfer knowledge is the key difference between traditional classroom and Web-based teaching. In traditional higher education, whether lab, classroom, advising, or research, faculty are with the learners and team members in time and space. The faculty member may have scripted the interaction, as in a lecture to three hundred students, but still has the ability to adjust the lesson in response to the audience of learners. Further, the faculty member may add new sections, devices, or materials at any time before or during the class or course. If a new journal article stimulates innovative ideas about the lesson or how to present the material, the instructor can quickly modify the course or project accordingly. Immediacy, relevance to current events, and the electricity of dynamic live performance—of trying something new—can add sparkle to the interaction between instructor and student.

Such immediacy is difficult, although not impossible, to achieve in Web-based instruction. Web-based instruction approaches that closely simulate face-to-face lecture, seminar, or lab are currently prohibitively expensive in dollars per student to produce, broadcast, and maintain when compared with on-site instruction (Phipps and Wellman, 2001). Models for sophisticated interactive, live, real-time learning experiences are found in small, grant- or industry-funded programs targeted to special audiences such as engineers. These models also require that students have technical sophistication and make large investments in technology hardware, software, and high-bandwidth Internet linkage if facilities are not provided by their college, university, or employer. Access is also currently limited to urban students because of the availability of high-speed communications infrastructure.

More typical Web-based instruction is the electronic analog of traditional print-based distance education, with one important difference: computer-mediated communication between learner and teacher, learner and administration staff, and learner and learner (American Association of University Professors, 1999; Marine, 2000). Computers and Web pages replace books, course readers, course manuals, postal service, and the telephone. Text with static graphics is the standard mode of transmitting course content (Eaton, 2001). Production costs, transmission costs, and limitations of communications networks (bandwidth) between the school, faculty member, and the learner make other transmission modes impractical (Phipps and Wellman, 2001).

Electronic communication is of critical importance in Web-mediated distance education. Students and faculty members report that their communications are essential in Web-mediated transfer of knowledge, but very time consuming (Marine, 2000; Young, 2000; Phipps and Wellman, 2001). Many faculty report that responding to learners' e-mails requires more time than preparation, presentation, and out-of-class interactions with students for classroom instruction. Delivering a Web-based course consumes as much time as conducting a daily seminar for ten to fifteen students for the duration of the course (Phipps and Wellman, 2001). Studies of student participants in distance education substantiate both the importance and increased frequency of student-instructor communications when compared with face-to-face instruction (American Association of University Professors, 1997; Phipps and Merisotis, 1999). Students report they are more comfortable asking questions for clarification or engaging the instructor in dialogue about content than in a traditional classroom (Marine, 2000).

Most faculty find that their task allocation shifts from preparation, presentation, and grading to intensive precourse preparation of modules and electronic-based materials, attention to student communications (e-mail, bulletin board, and chat room, as well as telephone, mail, and in-person), assignment and evaluation work, and course updating. As one faculty member said: "It's like writing a book while teaching courses and producing a new course, all at once . . . . And, as soon as you get it ready and start teaching, you start updating, which is very different from updating a lecture or classroom course because the technology is changing so rapidly and reprogramming takes a lot of effort, too . . . . The emails take me at least an hour every morning and every evening, then there are assignments to grade and feedback to each student" (Marine, 2000, 7).

Data for the delivery process includes completed assignments, frequency of Web-page access, patterns of use, frequency and types of constituent and faculty communications, modes of content delivery and frequency of their use, and quantitative and qualitative data on knowledge transfer, such as cognitive knowledge, skills, and decision making of learners.

Systems evaluation of Web-work will assist faculty and administrators in defining the effectiveness of the transformation of inputs, through specific functions of process, into specifically related outcomes. The evaluation should involve mapping individual faculty Web-work and determining where data are generated naturally in that process. Each process should be compared with others within the unit, within the discipline across units, and outside the discipline. Data often reside at points where building blocks or tasks for the project are completed and either sent to other people, assessed for usefulness, or added to the next step in the process. Not all data are equally important in determining effectiveness. Only data about task completions without which the project processes could not continue should be collected. For example, if a single graphic could not be made or is late, the instructor may simply tell students to refer to the textbook rather than take the time and effort to reproduce the one graphic on-line. If the content outline for Lesson 1 is not completed, however, the whole process stops until that critical task is completed, because order of presentation, graphical interface, development of instructional resources (including hyperlinked electronic sources), Web-page construction programming, and marketing support rely on that data.

Outcomes

The meaning of Web-work in evaluations for promotion and tenure, resource allocation, intellectual property rights, compensation, and constituent feedback remains uncertain in institutions using traditional systems of evaluation. Use of non-tenure-track instructors further complicates the evaluation of the effectiveness of Web-work. The institutions I studied have not revised traditional assessment processes to account for difference in time and effort, use of resources, and processes (such as Web sites, audiovisual communication objects/files, and daily e-mail interactions) to evaluate efficiency and effectiveness of faculty Web-work.

Faculty doing Web-work, particularly those seeking tenure or promotion, may well need to teach their chairs, deans, and colleagues what Web-work entails and what it accomplishes. Faculty should be ready to provide evidence for the effectiveness of their work in producing outcomes desired by their departments and institutions. Faculty should also identify and collect data that reflect their allocations of time, effort, and resources (equipment, supplies, work with other people, facilities, and finances) in the design, development, and delivery of Web-work. I recommend the use of a personal information manager (such as the Palm package, MS Outlook, Act!, and others) to create and maintain daily records of resources used for design, development, and delivery processes. Records should always include time, type of resource, and the target outcome.

Departments and institutions should also identify and collect data about each faculty member engaged in Web-work, resources necessary to accomplish the work, how each critical function is accomplished, and what is produced. I recommend creation of a common server-based database, standardized across units in the institution. Each unit should enter data about specific projects, including resources used, time on project, people engaged, and brief, pertinent comments that provide insight into adaptations to processes, changes in deadlines, or additional resources required. Data collection from Web-server logs can provide important information about learner or consumer patterns of access, navigation, and use of the delivery mechanisms.

Faculty Web-work continues to develop in ways that are both exciting and problematic for faculty who are hoping to reach broader audiences and engage in the most current modes of teaching, research, and service. Faculty and institutions should collaborate in designing and implementing systems evaluations of Web-work to ensure that decisions about faculty work, curricula, and institutional policy and resource allocation for Web-work are grounded in solid information.

References

American Association of University Professors. "Committee R on Government Relations Report on Distance Learning." [http://www.aup.org/govrel/distlern/dlrpttxt.htm]. Nov. 14, 1997.

American Association of University Professors. *Statement on Distance Education.* Washington, D.C.: American Association of University Professors, 1999.

Eaton, J. S. *Maintaining the Delicate Balance: Distance Learning, Higher Education Accreditation, and the Politics of Self-Regulation.* Washington, D.C.: American Council on Education, 2001.

Ford, D. H., and Lerner, R. M. *Developmental Systems Theory: An Integrative Approach.* Newbury Park, Calif.: Sage, 1992.

Green, K. C. *The Roads Behind and the Paths Ahead.* Claremont, Calif.: Claremont Graduate University, 1998. (ED 426718)

Green, K. C. *Campus Computing, 2000: The 11th National Survey of Computing and Information Technology in American Higher Education.* Encino, Calif.: Campus Computing, 2001. (ED 451744)

Marine, R. J. *Evaluation Research of Faculty Web-Work in a University Distance Education System: A Case Study of Effectiveness Using Qualitative and Quantitative Methods.* Unpublished consultation report, Julian, Penn., June 2000.

National Center for Education Statistics. "Distance Education at Postsecondary Institutions, 1997–98." [http://nces.ed.gov/pubs2000/2000013.pdf]. Dec. 1999.

National Center for Education Statistics. "Distance Education Instruction by Postsecondary Faculty and Staff, Fall 1998." [http://nces.ed.gov/pubs2002/2002155.pdf]. Feb. 2002.

Phipps, R., and Merisotis, J. *What's the Difference: A Review of Contemporary Research on the Effectiveness of Distance Learning in Higher Education.* Washington, D.C.: Institute for Higher Education Policy, 1999.

Phipps, R., and Wellman, J. *Funding the "Infostructure": A Guide to Financing Technology Infrastructure in Higher Education.* New Agenda Series, 3(2). Indianapolis, Ind.: Lumina Foundation, 2001.

Roche, J. "Checking The Radar: Survey Identifies Key IT Issues." *EDUCAUSE Quarterly,* 2000, 2, 4–9.

Russell, A. B. *State Perspectives on Higher Education Faculty Issues.* Washington, D.C.: State Higher Education Executive Officers, 2000.

Smullyan, R. M. *Theory of Formal Systems.* Princeton, N.J.: Princeton University Press, 1961.

Young, J. "David Noble's Battle to Defend the 'Sacred Space' of the Classroom." *Chronicle of Higher Education,* Mar. 31, 2000, p. A47.

ROBERT J. MARINE is assistant professor of anesthesiology and director, medical education research and development, at the Pennsylvania State University College of Medicine.

National and campus discussions about what should count in faculty evaluation have helped broaden the idea of scholarship at many colleges and universities, but for faculty who wish to fashion careers that include new kinds of scholarly work, debates about actual cases for tenure and promotion matter the most.

Faculty Evaluation and the Development of Academic Careers

Mary Taylor Huber

Academic careers in the United States are profoundly shaped by the expectations for scholarly accomplishment at the colleges and universities where faculty work. From graduate school to retirement, doors open or close depending on how well a scholar's efforts are regarded by colleagues at their own institution and by respected disciplinary peers. This fact of academic life underwrites the integrity and vitality of the intellectual enterprise. However, it also underlies the persistent dilemma of how to shape an academic career without "careerism"—worrying more about the rate than the quality of publication; waiting until after tenure to pursue an interest in teaching; delaying the start of a family. How can institutions help faculty set appropriate agendas and improve performance without compromising the intellectual values that give the profession its authenticity and attraction or the civic and human values that sustain personal and community life?

Although conflicts between academic success, intellectual integrity, and personal life date back to the establishment of the professional career path in American universities in the late nineteenth century (Bledstein, 1976), the issue has special currency in the heated world of higher education today. Over the past thirty years, postdoctorate, part-time, and full-time non-tenure-track positions have multiplied; competition for traditional full-time tenure-track positions has intensified; and faculty evaluation systems have become more formal and complex (Finkelstein, Seal, and Schuster, 1998; Braskamp and Ory, 1994; Diamond, 1999; Arreola, 2000). There is a sense that the bar for entry and promotion into academic careers has been rising rapidly, and there is concern that this trend will intensify as demands for social and financial accountability increase (Wilson, 2001; Altbach, 2000). Never has faculty work been so closely examined and never have the stakes in the quality of that examination seemed higher not only for individual scholars but also for the students, institutions, and communities that faculty serve.

Bringing faculty evaluation systems into line with current realities has become a priority nationwide. For example, the American Council on Education and the American Association of University Professors recently issued a report on the how-tos of tenure evaluation, recommending clarity in standards and procedures, consistency over time among candidates with different personal characteristics, candor in the evaluation of tenure-track faculty, and care for unsuccessful candidates (2000). Advocates for non-tenure-track faculty have raised the question of who should be evaluated, arguing that the professional respect and development that evaluation can foster should extend to all academic staff (Baldwin and Chronister, 2000). Faculty development professionals concerned with enhancing individual as well as institutional performance keep *why* questions engaged (see Braskamp and Ory, 1994, pp. 2–26), while the debate about posttenure review has brought the topic of when to evaluate center stage (American Association of University Professors, 1997; Licata and Morreale, 1997).

Although these how, who, why, and when issues all bear on the development of faculty careers, this chapter focuses on whether what counts in faculty evaluation is what is worthwhile. I will start with the recent national discussions about redefining *scholarship*, move on to campus policies and dilemmas, and finally turn to specific cases where faculty have followed a less-than-conventional path. In the end, I argue that national- and campus-level discussions about what should count in faculty evaluation have helped broaden the idea of scholarship at many colleges and universities but that debates about actual cases matter the most.

Defining *Scholarship* Strategically

The national discussion about broadening the definition of *scholarship* has traveled far since 1990, when Ernest Boyer urged that the meaning of the term be "creatively reconsidered." Boyer argued that the academy would have to recognize and reward a wide range of scholarly activity if it wished to tap the full range of faculty talent and fulfill its traditional missions of teaching, research, and service. The scholarships of discovery, integration, application, and teaching that he sketched out in *Scholarship Reconsidered* have entered the lexicon of higher education. Over a decade later, a consensus is growing that if these activities are to take root in faculty evaluation, the definition of scholarship will have to be sharpened once again. This does not return to the narrow connotation of scholarship as productivity in basic research. Rather, the effort now is to be more precise about what scholarship looks like in a wider range of activities, how to make this work available for peer review, and what criteria and standards are appropriate for its review.

A good place to start is with Robert Diamond's extraordinary effort with the scholarly and professional societies in the early 1990s to imagine what a broadened definition of scholarship might include. Historians, mathematicians, geographers, sociologists, chemists, architects, and professors in the visual and performing arts, business, and journalism all proposed frameworks to encompass the full range of scholarly work in their field. When the dust settled and the reports came out in *The Disciplines Speak*, almost all the participating societies agreed that scholarship meant more than the published results of basic research (Diamond and Adam, 1995, 2000).

To be sure, not everyone was on board. The American Academy of Religion was "not at all sanguine that redefining the word scholarship to cover teaching or other professional activities now not normally considered as such is particularly useful or appropriate" (1995, p. 19). But even those associations that did propose more inclusive definitions sensed that something more precise was needed. For example, the Joint Policy Board for Mathematics stated: "The results of scholarly activities must be public and must be amenable to evaluation" (1995, p. 66). In addition, the American Chemical Society had stated in 1993: "The task force recognizes the fact that mechanisms for gauging scholarship in areas outside of research are not generally or firmly in place. We encourage the creative development of new approaches to measure scholarship in chemistry across a broad spectrum of activities" (2000, p. 47).

This is where The Carnegie Foundation's second report on faculty work, *Scholarship Assessed*, came in (Glassick, Huber, and Maeroff, 1997). Introduced by Ernest Boyer at the American Association for Higher Education's (AAHE) Forum on Faculty Roles and Rewards in 1994 and completed by his colleagues in 1997, the report proposed six standards by which scholarship across a broad spectrum of activities could be identified and its quality judged. Could scholarship be broadly defined? Yes, the authors said, it is appropriate to apply the term to any of the academic functions *Scholarship Reconsidered* had identified, provided they are undertaken and performed as serious intellectual work. Could we sharpen that definition? Yes, serious intellectual work in discovery, integration, application, or teaching is marked by clear goals, adequate preparation, appropriate methods, significant results, effective presentation, and reflective critique (including peer review).

Scholarship Assessed was certainly not alone. A good number of people were working throughout the 1990s to sharpen the definition of scholarship in their particular domains. Lee Shulman's influential article, "Teaching as Community Property," published in *Change* in 1993, argued that scholarly work must be public and available for colleagues to critique and build upon—an insight that Shulman, Pat Hutchings, Russ Edgerton, and their colleagues developed and elaborated in AAHE's Peer Review of Teaching Project and the Course Portfolio Project (see Shulman, 1996; Hutchings, 1996, 1998). The scholarship of integration—at least in the guise of public scholarship—received a great deal of attention in the academic community and the intellectual press during the mid-1990s (Bender, 1993; Boynton, 1995; Garrison, Jones, Pollack, and Said, 1995). And Ernest Lynton provided the benchmark arguments for the scholarship of application (or engagement) in his 1995 book *Making the Case for Professional Service* and its sequel by Amy Driscoll and Ernie Lynton, *Making Outreach Visible* (1999).

A vigorous national discussion continues about what should count as scholarship and on how faculty evaluation can take account of a wider range of academic work. Integrative and applied scholarships have been receiving new attention through the Urban Universities Portfolio Project and by such universities as Michigan State, Nebraska, and Indiana University. Indeed, Indiana University's new report on service suggests that quality indicators like impact and significance, intellectual work, and communication and interaction are applicable not only to engagement and outreach but to professional and institutional citizenship (1999), while the Associated New American Colleges are extending the criteria suggested in *Scholarship Assessed* to governance and institutional service (Berberet, 1999). Public and private foundations, the higher education associations, scholarly societies and accrediting agencies are spurring a great deal of thoughtful work in science curricula and pedagogy; teaching, learning, and technology; the assessment of student learning; and the documentation and evaluation of teaching. The concept of the scholarship of teaching itself is undergoing further exploration and development. In particular, The Carnegie Foundation, under its new president, Lee Shulman, has organized a national fellowship program and an associated set of campus academies for scholars who want to approach teaching in a spirit of inquiry, with questions about learning in mind (Hutchings and Shulman, 1999; Cambridge, 2001).

Campus Policies and Dilemmas

Expectations for scholarly accomplishment on campus have the most effect in shaping faculty careers. Official guidelines for faculty roles and rewards have expanded to embrace a broader view of faculty work. When The Carnegie Foundation surveyed provosts at four-year colleges and universities in 1994, some 80 percent said that they had either recently reexamined their systems of faculty roles and rewards or planned to do so soon (Glassick, Huber, and Maeroff, 1997, pp. 12–14). Of those institutions that had already completed or initiated this process, 86 percent reported that redefining faculty roles had been a focus of their review and 78 percent said that the definition of scholarship was being broadened to include the full range of activities in which faculty are engaged. For example, 54 percent said that applied scholarship (outreach) was being clearly distinguished from campus and community citizenship activity, while 80 percent claimed that the definition of teaching was being broadened to include such work as curriculum development, advising, and conducting instructional and classroom research.

A few colleges and universities have actually written *Scholarship Reconsidered*'s four categories of scholarship into their guidelines for promotion and tenure, while many others have modified existing categories to reflect a broader view (O'Meara, 2000, pp. 156–157). Oregon State University, for example, started with discussion of *Scholarship Reconsidered*, which evolved into a definition of scholarship as "intellectual work whose significance is validated by peers and which is communicated. More specifically, such work in its diverse forms is based on a high level of professional expertise; must give evidence of originality; must be documented and validated as through peer review or critique; and must be communicated in appropriate ways so as to have impact on or significance for publics beyond the University, or for the discipline itself. Intellectual work in teaching is scholarship," the guidelines continue, "if it is shared with peers in journals, in formal presentations at professional meetings, or in comparable peer-evaluated forms" (Oregon State University, 2000; see also Weiser, 1997). Some institutions are experimenting with arrangements similar to the "creativity contract" that *Scholarship Reconsidered* had proposed. At Kent State University in Ohio, for example, the College of Nursing recognizes that "the scholarship of discovery, integration, application and teaching are integral parts of the College of Nursing's Faculty Scholarship" and allows faculty members to choose particular emphases for their work. While all tenure-track faculty are expected to show continued growth in the scholarship of discovery or integration, "faculty with a primary emphasis on teaching will have higher weighing placed on the scholarship of teaching. Faculty with a primary emphasis on research will have higher weighing placed on the scholarhip of discovery/application/integration" (Kent State University College of Nursing, 1996, p. E1.2).

Still, the effect of the new zeitgeist, not to mention the new rules and regulations, remains uncertain. On the one hand, survey results indicate renewed emphasis on teaching, especially at doctoral institutions. Robert Diamond and Bronwyn Adam's work on shifting priorities between research and undergraduate teaching at research and doctoral universities showed that in eight of the eleven institutions they surveyed in 1996–1997, "faculty, department chairs' and deans' perceptions about their institutions have shifted away from a research emphasis toward a balance between teaching and research" (1997, p. 1). Indeed, The Carnegie Foundation's 1997 national survey of college and university faculty survey suggests that a greater emphasis is being given to teaching in research universities nationwide: nearly half (45 percent) of faculty at these institutions said that teaching counts more now for purposes of faculty advancement than it did five years ago.

On the other hand, there is a dark side to this story. A sizable proportion of research university faculty said that although teaching counted more, the demands for research and creative work had not diminished (25 percent) or had risen at the same time (11 percent). Some even reported that although the importance of teaching remains the same, the importance of research has risen (11 percent). Faculty at other types of institutions tell a similar story. A quarter of the respondents at doctoral universities, 23 percent at master's colleges and universities, 19 percent at baccalaureate colleges, and 18 percent at associate-of-arts colleges say that teaching counts more than it did before. Interestingly, at the four-year institutions, an even larger number of faculty report that research demands have been rising: 42 percent at doctoral universities, 41 percent at masters colleges and universities, and 35 percent at baccalaureate colleges. For many faculty, these are intersecting demands. Overall, 27 percent of all the nation's college and university professors say that both teaching and research count more than they did five years ago or that one counts more while the other counts the same (see Huber, 1998).

As my coauthors and I observed in *Scholarship Assessed,* reform seldom moves evenly on all fronts. Policies are being rewritten, new perspectives are making integrative and applied scholarship more acceptable, teaching is getting greater weight, and the scholarship of teaching is beginning to gain credibility. These innovations help create a climate of support for scholars who wish to broaden their range and improve their work. However, there is concern that already overworked faculty are coming under pressure to do more. Some educators worry, too, that heightened scrutiny within our increasingly managerial colleges and universities may lead to a loss of the kind of autonomy that has long contributed to the attraction of academic life (Clark, 1997; Gumport, 1997). Finally, many faculty still perceive a disconnect between policy and practice and consider the real measure of success to lie in how well the various forms of scholarship fare in appointment, promotion, tenure, and annual reviews.

Faculty Evaluation and Academic Careers

Scholarship gains specific meaning less in rules and regulations than in deliberations about particular cases, which all—at least potentially—involve questions about the nature of a faculty member's accomplishments, the level of distinction of those accomplishments, and how much of what kind of work is enough. These cases influence academic careers both by deciding the fate of individuals for appointment, reappointment, tenure, or promotion—and by the messages these decisions send to faculty who are setting agendas or helping others to do so through "corridor talk" and advice. (See Downey, Dumit, and Traweek, 1997.) This is often how news about change enters the system, for example, that it may now take two books instead of one for tenure, that large grants are now necessary for promotion, that college or university service is or is not likely to count for much, or that new kinds of scholarship acknowledged in the revised guidelines may not, in fact, actually get rewarded.

Consider the case of a young chemist from a metropolitan university. Her institution had recently spent two years redefining its mission and inviting its faculty to integrate their work in teaching, research, and service toward improving the quality of urban life. With broad interests in chemistry education, this assistant professor became the university's new poster child. When it was time for tenure and she received the official notebook for presenting her case, she tore out the dividers labeled "teaching," "research," and "service" and reorganized her material to emphasize the integrated nature of her work. In a remarkable session at the American Association for Higher Education's 1998 Forum on Faculty Roles and Rewards, a panel from that institution, including the associate vice chancellor, faculty head of the campuswide promotion and tenure committee, chair of the chemistry teaching and research committee, and the young chemist herself, made clear that although her case embodied official university ideals, it also challenged the existing tenure criteria, which were still written in terms of excellence in research, teaching, and service. This case became highly contentious, generating much discussion about the nature of scholarship at the institution, and the chemist won by a very slim margin. But when asked whether she would advise others to follow her path, she said, "No, not in a thousand years."

Street knowledge like this sometimes finds its way into print. Indeed, there is now a whole genre of guides—often well-meaning, often mildly if not severely cynical—to the realities rather than the pieties of academic advancement (see, for example, Boice, 2000; Goodstein and Woodward, 1999; Machiavelli [Hitt], 1993). Who knows the impact of this literature? Surely, however, the most effective mode of keeping aspirants on the straight and narrow trail is advice that travels orally from friend to friend, senior colleague to junior colleague, and mentor to mentee. Lack of an effective network has often been considered a handicap for women and minorities entering the system (Aisenberg and Harrington, 1988). Academics who are fortunate enough to have good mentors, however, learn early and often the risks of taking a less-traveled road.

My current research involves developing case studies of faculty at research universities who have made the scholarship of teaching part of their academic careers (Huber, 2001). This work is turning up well-meaning warnings against even conventional research agendas that seem not quite opportune. For example, a psychologist recalls advice that he received while still a graduate student: "a Polonius-like conversation with a . . . wonderful experimental psychologist, who was on my dissertation committee. And as I was leaving, he said, 'you've got to stop doing that research you're doing. It's too slow . . . . Do something quick. Get it out. Get tenure, and then you can go back and do the things you think are important.'" The mentor of another subject recalls advising him—begging him—to put his time as an assistant professor into publishing his dissertation research in a book and articles rather than pursuing his interests in pedagogy and humanities computing. As she said, "it's become the case that it's research that really turns the tide. I mean, no matter what the policies are or what's in print, it really does come down to [conventional] scholarship."

Convention, however, can be used to frame a not entirely conventional career. A chemistry professor at a large Midwestern university made a successful bid for tenure on the basis of accomplishments in curriculum reform, evaluation, and innovative pedagogies providing opportunities for undergraduates to *teach*. He and his mentors had realized that his tenure case would be strongest if his work could be judged by the usual standards, and the strategy worked. He won external grants to support research on the effectiveness of his program, published articles in refereed journals about his pedagogical research, lectured and led workshops around the country, networked extensively, and achieved national recognition as a chemistry educator. When it was time to submit materials, he divided his accomplishments in the general area of teaching and learning between the university's traditional categories of "teaching" and "research." His teaching stood out for its innovation, documentation, and recognition, while his research made sense in very conventional terms as an accumulation of grants, projects, publications, and invitations, all vouched for by prestigious referees.

Although this chemist is a strong advocate of making the case for scholarship in teaching in traditional terms, some people are using what he calls "the language of exception" to claim new directions for scholarly careers. The pioneer in humanities computing, mentioned previously, became too engaged in new media work to follow his mentor's advice to publish conventionally and let his colleagues decide whether the innovative electronic environments he had designed for scholars and students in American Studies could or should be considered tenurable scholarly work. An engineering professor with nationally recognized contributions in engineering education reform let her colleagues decide whether her traditional research record was heightened or diminished by her pedagogical work. By all accounts, both were edgy cases. Yet both scholars won.

But they did not win only for themselves. Indeed, their cases still reverberate through their larger campus and disciplinary communities, giving hope to those who follow. Not all have been successful. But as one engineering professor told me, he uses stories like these to advise his mentees that although there are risks, they can "be what they are, be courageous, be brave and follow their ideas and do the right thing. . . . I have not advised them to just do research and then later when they're successful, then they can start doing teaching. No. Not at all. What I've advised is that there has to be balance."

Conclusion

Faculty evaluation influences academic careers through decisions that seal the fate of individuals while also sending powerful messages about what exactly—in a particular environment—*scholarship* can mean. Certainly, these cases underline the importance of constructing arguments for engaging in a broader range of scholarship with great care, given the ambiguity that still surrounds the term. More specifically, they underline the importance of developing genres like course portfolios through which to demonstrate, share, and critique scholarship in classroom teaching, because this—even more than research on teaching or leadership in curriculum and materials development—is still new and unfamiliar ground. They also underline the importance of engaging in the kind of debate outlined by *Scholarship Assessed* concerning what standards might be used to assure the quality of scholarly work of all kinds.

When the topic is faculty evaluation, the debates that matter most are those concerned with the particulars of individual cases. But this is not to say that other levels of debate do not matter. Clearly, they do. Debates about the kinds and quality of faculty work that take place in the higher education press, in scholarly society meetings, in the faculty senate, in department meetings, and even in the hallways all inform the actual cases for tenure and promotion that people are able to make for themselves or their colleagues. And in turn, as more people are successful in making such cases—and careers—on the basis of broader notions of scholarship, others will be strengthened in their resolve to do so as well.

Acknowledgments

I am grateful to Randy Bass, Dan Bernstein, Brian Coppola, Doris Kimbrough, Sheri Sheppard, and their colleagues for speaking so frankly and openly about their careers (see also Bass, 1999; Huber, 2001).

References

Aisenberg, N., and Harrington, M. *Women of Academe: Outsiders in the Sacred Grove.* Amherst: University of Massachusetts Press, 1988.
Altbach, P. G. "The Deterioration of the Academic Estate: International Patterns of Academic Work." In P. G. Altbach (ed.), *The Changing Academic Workplace.* Boston: Center for International Higher Education, School of Education, Boston College, 2000.
American Academy of Religion. "Religious Studies and the Redefining Scholarship Project." In R. M. Diamond and B. E. Adam (eds.), *The Disciplines Speak.* Washington, D.C.: American Association for Higher Education, 1995.
American Association of University Professors. "On Post-tenure Review." *Academe* 1997, *83*(5), 44–51.
American Chemical Society. "Report of the Task Force on the Definition of Scholarship in Chemistry, 1993." Reprinted in B. E. Adam and A. Roberts, "Differences Among

the Disciplines." In R. M. Diamond and B. E. Adam (eds.), *Recognizing Faculty Work: Reward Systems for the Year 2000.* San Francisco: Jossey-Bass, 2000.

American Council on Education, American Association of University Professors, and United Educators Insurance Risk Retention Group. *Good Practice in Tenure Evaluation: Advice for Tenured Faculty, Department Chairs, and Academic Administrators.* Washington, D.C.: American Council on Education, 2000.

Arreola, R. *Developing a Comprehensive Faculty Evaluation System.* (2nd ed.) Bolton, Mass.: Anker, 2000.

Baldwin, R. G., and Chronister, J. L. *Teaching Without Tenure: Policies and Practices for a New Era.* Baltimore: Johns Hopkins University Press, 2000.

Bass, R. "Discipline and Publish: Faculty Work, Technology, and Accountability." Plenary Address, Seventh AAHE Forum on Faculty Roles and Rewards, San Diego, Calif., 1999. [http://www.georgetown.edu/bassr/disc&pub.html].

Bender, T. *Intellect and Public Life: Essays on the Social History of Academic Intellectuals in the United States.* Baltimore: Johns Hopkins University Press, 1993.

Berberet, J. "The Professoriate and Institutional Citizenship: Toward a Scholarship of Service." *Liberal Education,* 1999, 85(4), 33–39.

Bledstein, B. J. *The Culture of Professionalism: The Middle Class and the Development of Higher Education in America.* New York: Norton, 1976.

Boice, R. *Advice for New Faculty Members.* Boston: Allyn & Bacon, 2000.

Boyer, E. L. *Scholarship Reconsidered: Priorities of the Professoriate.* Princeton, N.J.: The Carnegie Foundation for the Advancement of Teaching, 1990.

Boynton, R. S. 1995. "The New Intellectuals." *Atlantic Monthly,* Mar. 1995, pp. 53–70.

Braskamp, L. A., and Ory, J. C. *Assessing Faculty Work: Enhancing Individual and Institutional Performance.* San Francisco: Jossey-Bass, 1994.

Cambridge, B. "Fostering the Scholarship of Teaching and Learning: Communities of Practice." In D. Lieberman and C. Wehlburg (eds.), *To Improve the Academy.* Vol. 19. Bolton, Mass.: Anker, 2001.

The Carnegie Foundation for the Advancement of Teaching. *The Carnegie Classification of Institutions of Higher Education, 2000 Edition.* Menlo Park, Calif.: The Carnegie Foundation for the Advancement of Teaching, 2000.

Clark, B. R. "Small Worlds, Different Worlds: The Uniqueness and Troubles of American Academic Professions." *Daedalus,* 1997, 126(4), 21–42.

Diamond, R. M. *Aligning Faculty Rewards with Institutional Mission: Statements, Policies, and Guidelines.* Bolton, Mass.: Anker, 1999.

Diamond, R. M., and Adam, B. E. *The Disciplines Speak: Rewarding the Scholarly, Professional, and Creative Work of Faculty.* Washington, D.C.: American Association for Higher Education, 1995.

Diamond, R. M., and Adam, B. E. *Changing Priorities at Research Universities: 1991–1996.* Syracuse, N.Y.: Center for Instructional Development, Syracuse University, 1997.

Diamond, R. M., and Adam, B. E. *The Disciplines Speak II: More Statements on Rewarding the Scholarly, Professional, and Creative Work of Faculty.* Washington, D.C.: American Association for Higher Education, 2000.

Downey, G. L., Dumit, J., and Traweek, S. "Corridor Talk." In G. L. Downey and J. Dumit (eds.), *Cyborgs and Citadels: Anthropological Interventions in Emerging Sciences and Technologies.* Santa Fe, N.M.: School of American Research Press, 1997.

Driscoll, A., and Lynton, E. A. *Making Outreach Visible: A Guide to Documenting Professional Service and Outreach.* Washington, D.C.: American Association for Higher Education, 1999.

Finkelstein, M. J., Seal, R. K., and Schuster, J. H. *The New Academic Generation: A Profession in Transformation.* Baltimore: Johns Hopkins University Press, 1998.

Garrison, G. R., Jones, A. A., Pollack, R., and Said, E. *Beyond the Academy: A Scholar's Obligations.* ACLS Occasional Paper, no. 31. New York: American Council of Learned Societies, 1995.

Glassick, C. E., Huber, M. T., and Maeroff, G. I. *Scholarship Assessed: Evaluation of the Professoriate.* San Francisco: Jossey Bass, 1997.

Goodstein, D., and Woodward, J. "Inside Science." *The American Scholar,* 1999, *68*(4), 83–90.

Gumport, P. J. "Public Universities as Academic Workplaces." *Daedalus,* 1997, *126*(4), 113–136.

Huber, M. T. *Community College Faculty: Attitudes and Trends, 1997.* Stanford, Calif.: National Center for Postsecondary Improvement, 1998.

Huber, M. T. "Balancing Acts: Designing Careers Around the Scholarship of Teaching." *Change,* 2001, *33*(4), 21–29.

Hutchings, P. *Making Teaching Community Property: A Menu for Peer Collaboration and Review.* Washington, D.C.: AAHE Teaching Initiative, American Association for Higher Education, 1996.

Hutchings, P. (ed.). *The Course Portfolio: How Faculty Can Examine Their Teaching to Advance Practice and Improve Student Learning.* Washington, D.C.: American Association for Higher Education, 1998.

Hutchings, P., and Shulman, L. S. "The Scholarship of Teaching: New Elaborations, New Developments." *Change,* 1999, *31*(5), 11–15.

Indiana University. *Service at Indiana University: Defining, Documenting, and Evaluating.* Indianapolis, Ind.: Strategic Directions Project on Professional Service, 1999.

Joint Policy Board for Mathematics. "Recognition and Rewards in the Mathematical Sciences, 1995." In R. M. Diamond and B. E. Adam (eds.), *The Disciplines Speak.* Washington, D.C.: American Association for Higher Education, 1995.

Kent State University College of Nursing. "Statement on Faculty Scholarship." In *College of Nursing Faculty Handbook.* Kent, Ohio: Kent State University College of Nursing, 1996.

Licata, C. M., and Morreale, J. C. *Post-tenure Review: Policies, Practices, and Precautions.* Washington, D.C.: American Association for Higher Education, 1997.

Lynton, E. A. *Making the Case for Professional Service.* Washington, D.C.: American Association for Higher Education, 1995.

Machiavelli, N. [J. Hitt]. "The Professor." *Lingua Franca,* July/Aug. 1993, cover, pp. 24–29.

O'Meara, K. A. "Climbing the Academic Ladder: Promotion in Rank." In C. A. Trower (ed.), *Policies on Faculty Appointment: Standard Practices and Unusual Arrangements.* Bolton, Mass.: Anker, 2000.

Oregon State University. "OSU Promotion and Tenure Guidelines." Guidelines approved 1995, revised 2000. [http://oregonstate.edu/facultystaff/handbook/promoten/spromoten.htm]. July 2, 2002.

Shulman, L. S. "Teaching as Community Property." *Change,* 1993, *25*(6), 6.

Shulman, L. S. "Course Anatomy: The Dissection and Analysis of Knowledge Through Teaching." In P. Hutchings (ed.), *The Course Portfolio.* Washington, D.C.: American Association for Higher Education, 1996.

Weiser, C. J. "Faculty Scholarship and Productivity Expectations: An Administrator's Perspective." *HortScience,* 1997, *32*(1), 37–39.

Wilson, R. "A Higher Bar for Earning Tenure." *Chronicle of Higher Education,* Jan. 5, 2001, pp. A12–13.

MARY TAYLOR HUBER *is a senior scholar at* The Carnegie Foundation for the Advancement of Teaching, *where she directs research on cultures of teaching in higher education. She is coauthor of* The Carnegie Foundation report Scholarship Assessed: Evaluation of the Professoriate.

8

*Targeted, action-oriented institutional research can help
a college or university better understand and more
effectively utilize faculty resources. This chapter profiles
one multicampus research university whose institutional
research portfolio has emphasized faculty issues.*

Institutional Research to Enhance Faculty Performance

Michael J. Dooris

This chapter illustrates several specific ways that one multicampus research university is selectively employing targeted, change-oriented institutional research (IR) about faculty performance. These efforts go beyond routine reports and factbook type information to improve understanding of the experiences of its faculty members, to enhance faculty development, and to use faculty resources more effectively.

Evolving Role of Institutional Research with Faculty Issues

Throughout the history of the field of institutional research, practitioners have reflected about what IR is and where it is headed. Volkwein (1999) provides a well-informed and concise overview of trends in the field. He notes that as institutional research offices have become more interwoven with strategic planning, continuous quality improvement, and assessment, they have become more entrepreneurial, collaborative, management-oriented, and aimed more deliberately at the improvement of critical institutional functions and processes at many colleges and universities.

There is virtually an unlimited array of legitimate and interesting questions that proactive and adaptive institutional research conceivably can address. It is fair to ask, "What are the areas in which targeted, management-oriented institutional research is likely to be most productive?" The answers to that question differ for different colleges and universities. Likely areas for institutional research include academic assessment, enrollment management, budgeting, diversity issues, technological change, changes in the postsecondary education industry, and development. Issues that can be loosely grouped under the heading of "faculty" deserve a place on such a list, and they have been a priority for IR at the university profiled in this chapter.

Faculty issues provide a potentially productive focus for targeted, action-oriented institutional research for two reasons. First, faculty and faculty work are at the core of a college or university. Redefinitions of faculty work roles, technology, and changing student and societal expectations are modifying the ways faculty do their work and the methods by which their performance is or should be evaluated. Therefore, faculty issues provide an opportunity for IR to play a significant positive role in informing institutional responses to the internal and external changes that will affect how well a college or university carries out its core mission. Second, on most campuses, there is a plethora of existing institutional data that are not fully utilized. Only a few of the examples described in this chapter require new (and relatively modest) data-gathering efforts. Institutional researchers can often unobtrusively tap much centrally held transactional-type data in human resources files, financial systems, and registrars' databases that have been collected and stored for other purposes. In some cases, they can use existing institutional data to benchmark against already available external data.

In brief, institutional research on faculty issues is important and feasible. This is an area in which carefully targeted, well-conceived, and effectively implemented institutional research can make a substantive contribution to the management of a college or university.

Practical IR Strategies

The usual guidelines, caveats, and advice about effective institutional research are as applicable to IR on faculty as to IR generally. A thorough review of the professional practice literature is outside the scope of this chapter—publications such as Middaugh, Trusheim, and Bauer (1994) and Whitely, Porter, and Fenske (1992) are comprehensive sources of suggestions and advice—but it is useful to emphasize a few ideas.

The IR office should be a central player in the management of and access to institutional databases. IR staff should build and maintain strong working relationships with personnel in related offices such as the registrar and the budget office. The IR office should also make connections across organizational silos—with academic affairs, student affairs, the graduate school, and deans' offices. Those connections are important, especially if IR begins to tread on what is traditionally considered academic or administrative terrain.

IR staff should look for opportunities to leverage existing data such as transcript files and human resources files. Transactional data used for administrative purposes tend to be reliable, and they provide unobtrusive data sources. Surveys, interviews, and focus groups can be useful as well. Occasional short, action-oriented data collection is far preferable to uncoordinated proliferation of lengthy and onerous surveys with no clear policy outcome.

In addition, institutional researchers should remember to keep reports to senior executives short, to the point, and focused on a few descriptive statistics, conclusions, and management implications. Underlying detail is often necessary and appropriate, of course, but analysts should deliver the punch line clearly and simply. H. L. Mencken satirized "an unshakable determination to tell it all" (Cooke, 1958, p. 45), and few presidents or provosts want to read an IR report of more than a couple of pages.

Institutional research on faculty issues demands a high level of what Terenzini (1999) calls "issues intelligence" and "contextual intelligence." Faculty and faculty work are at the core of colleges and universities, so the institutional researcher exploring workload, promotion and tenure data, productivity, and evaluation and reward systems is venturing into deep organizational waters. He or she should have a fairly strong contextual understanding of higher education generally and also possess a relatively well-developed sensitivity to the culture, climate, processes, and values (both formal and informal) of his or her campus.

Before initiating specialized analyses, an institution should routinize the tabulation of basic organizational self-knowledge of the sort typically found in a factbook or in program and performance indicators: faculty tenure, rank, and appointment type; student credit hour production; annual faculty salary reports; and so on. A well-organized system for periodic (typically annual) production and dissemination of these reports should be in place before an IR office undertakes more specialized and targeted analyses such as those that follow about faculty-issues institutional research to support adaptation and improvement.

Instructional Workload

The core business of a college or university is teaching and learning, and the core employees are faculty members. Effective and efficient performance at any college or university—public or private, small or large—therefore hinges to a considerable extent on how well it uses faculty resources for instruction.

It can be difficult to measure how well a college is carrying out this critical aspect of its mission. For example, research suggests that trustees, administrators, and faculty leaders typically think of productivity in two ways—efficiency or quality—and these are frequently seen as inherently in conflict (Birnbaum, 1992). One such conflict emerges in the trade-offs involved in small class size or the use of part-time faculty. Campus leaders have a limited ability to affect the wide assortment of relevant faculty issues—hiring, retention, salary and rewards, workload assignments, professional development, productivity, and mentoring. Constraints include environmental pressures, political processes, an institution's history, its culture, and leadership style. A lack of data is seldom the only problem or even the main problem.

For these reasons, an institutional researcher, even a seasoned practitioner, should dip into the literature before embarking on workload studies. Middaugh, Trusheim, and Bauer (1994, pp. 80–90) and Wergin (1994) offer digestible, pragmatic advice on the analysis of workload. Meyer (1998) reviews faculty workload studies from fifteen states, discussing the findings, the policy implications, and the conceptual and definitional problems. Massy and Zemsky (1994) and Rosovsky (1992) raise important conceptual, political, and organizational considerations, but they are relatively abstract and probably will not provide models that IR offices will follow for reports on their individual campuses.

Meaningful and usable instructional analyses can be deceptively complex, and simplistic approaches taken in isolation are not likely to be helpful. Lack of usable workload data developed according to institution-wide definitions and conventions only makes a difficult situation more ambiguous. The case study university created a faculty instructional workload model in 1997 that at least partially addresses these issues. The model is accessible to senior administrators (the provost, all deans, and selected other individuals) via a secure Web server. It displays all formal teaching assignments for all standing and non–standing appointment faculty.

The inputs to the model are unobtrusive, coming from existing data bases such as the registrar's master file of course offerings and the payroll file. No surveys are needed, and no new data are collected. Because the model is Web-based, institutional research staff avoid the practical limitations of a printed report. (A complete copy of the instructional workload analysis output for one semester would require about one thousand pages in a print version.)

The model provides information at the all-university, college, campus, and department levels, right down to the individual faculty member. The provost can access the model on-line and click on all courses and sections taught by any faculty member in any department of the university. The model presents data on the following elements, by semester and by course level (that is, lower-division undergraduate, upper-division undergraduate, and graduate courses):

- Appointment type (full-time standing, full-time single-year, and so on)
- Rank (professor, associate professor, and so on)
- Resident instruction full-time equivalent faculty member (FTE, based on budgeted salary splits)
- Number of standard sections taught (including regular teaching assignments and factors in shared assignments such as team-teaching but excluding dissertation advising and supervision of independent study)

- Number of credit hours
- Enrollment (graduate, undergraduate, and total)

At the university's largest campus, the model shows that, on average, faculty have formal instructional responsibility for about 2.4 standard sections per resident instruction FTE each semester, with about 5.7 credit hours per semester. In other words, the average faculty member at that campus teaches about two three-credit courses per semester. There is considerable variation among appointment types, colleges, and campuses.

The model has been in place for about three years. It continues to be refined as administrators and IR staff learn together what is and is not useful. Some of these lessons have been counter-intuitive. For example, an early version of the model highlighted data on instructors who are paid to teach (that is, faculty who are on instructional budgets) but who have no formal teaching assignments. This description fits perhaps 150 faculty in any given semester in a university with 2,500 tenure-line faculty. This situation seemed to offer potential for significant productivity improvement. We discovered, however, numerous special situations, such as professors creating new courses, coordinating (but not teaching) large undergraduate programs such as freshmen calculus, developing new tutoring centers, or overseeing new study abroad programs. We learned that these special situations are legitimate and not worth ongoing effort to monitor, investigate, and justify.

The model is useful because it provides a common basis for informed conversations between a provost and deans or between a dean and department heads about instructional workload and about the factors involved in the workload assignment process in academic units. A model like this makes it possible—easy, even—for academic administrators to compare teaching loads in two departments, using accurate, audited, and uniform institutional data, and to consider which units may be understaffed and therefore in need of more faculty lines to cope with heavy instructional demands. The model in itself does not and should not resolve debates or make decisions. There are legitimate differences among disciplines and among college, departmental, and campus missions. There is no substitute for judgment and interpretation. But an instructional workload model like this is a feasible and practical IR tool that provides enhanced information for those conversations.

Tenure Progression

The debate over tenure involves complex and sometimes heated ideological arguments.

"Tenure has become the academy's version of the abortion issue—a controversy marked by passion, polemics, and hardened convictions" (Chait, 1997, p. B4). A survey of almost 34,000 faculty members at 378 colleges and universities found 38 percent agreeing, "Tenure is an outmoded concept." However, the same survey found 54 percent agreeing with "Tenure is essential to attract the best minds to academe" (Sax and others, 1999).

The tenure-progression model was begun at the case study university in 1998 at the instigation of the vice provost responsible for academic personnel. The model tracks new entrants to the tenure track over a seven-year period. Seven years includes the normal probationary period plus one year to accurately reflect the experience of tenure candidates who stopped the clock, usually for maternity leave or illness. At the time this chapter is written, four such cohorts have been tracked, as summarized in Table 8.1.

There were 103 new entrants to provisional status university-wide in the 1993 cohort. Seven years later, 55 of these individuals (53 percent) had been awarded tenure. Those who did not achieve tenure generally had ended their university employment, although a very few continued employment in nontenured positions such as staff jobs. Overall, for the four cohorts studied to date, the percentage of faculty achieving tenure is 57 percent, and there are differences by gender and ethnicity. The complete institutional analysis includes year-by-year detail for each cohort and data by campus, college, and other demographic groups.

This might seem fundamental information, but it is missing on many campuses. As noted by Chait (1997, p. B4), "Academics normally insist on empirical evidence and factual data, yet the debate on tenure often proceeds without either. To a remarkable degree, universities lack basic information. . . . Why not collect and publish annually data—by race, gender, and department or school—on how many faculty members achieve tenure?"

The tenure-progression analysis provides descriptive information to the vice provost for academic affairs, who shares it annually with the university's council of academic deans and with the faculty senate, and periodically in other forums such as a board of trustee workshop or a peer institution meeting. With solid data, administrators can answer claims that the tenure system is unfair or that tenure standards are too lax, while working from an informed position to improve institutional personnel policies and practices.

Table 8.1.   Tenure Progression for Four Faculty Cohorts, by Year of Entry to Tenure Track

	Entrants	Tenured After 7 Years	Overall Rate (%)	Female	Rate (%)	Minority	Rate (%)
1990 cohort	121	70	57	19/40	48	9/18	50
1991 cohort	93	55	59	15/30	50	5/8	63
1992 cohort	151	89	59	28/55	51	15/29	52
1993 cohort	103	55	53	12/31	39	8/17	47
4-year totals	468	269	57	74/156	47	37/72	51

Source: Center for Quality and Planning, annual reports, 1998–2001.

Exit Surveys and Interviews

The IR models described previously provide quantitative data about the numbers and percentages of faculty achieving tenure and the numbers of students and courses they are teaching. They do not address broader questions about faculty experiences, priorities, culture, roles, and rewards, such as those raised in influential books such as Boyer's *Scholarship Reconsidered* (1990), Glassick, Huber, and Maeroff's *Scholarship Assessed* (1997), and Fairweather's *Faculty Work and Public Trust* (1996).

The vice provost for academic affairs at the case study university initiated a faculty exit study process in 1997–98. With IR support, the process offers every tenured and tenure-track faculty member leaving the opportunity to participate in an exit survey and interview. This is done with the help of each academic dean at the institution. In 1999–2000, the study was conducted for the third consecutive year.

Faculty exit interview officers, appointed by the respective colleges, conduct the interviews. With respondents' permission, they share their written reports of individual interviews with the respective dean and with the vice provost for academic affairs. Survey results are tabulated centrally and anonymously. Use of these two measures has several advantages. The interviews provide the opportunity for exiting faculty to speak (at least indirectly) to their deans on the record, while the surveys provide confidentiality and cross-university quantitative data.

In 1999–2000, 107 provisional and tenured faculty exited employment. Approximately two-thirds of that population responded through at least one of the two mechanisms. There were fifty-seven exit interviews and thirty-six responses to the exit survey. The exact response rate is unknown; overlap in these two response sets is uncertain, because written survey responses allowed anonymity. Nine faculty members declined to participate in the process in any way. Another six said they would participate in the interview but not the written instrument, while four agreed only to the anonymous written instrument. The participation rate was the same as a year earlier. A few comments from the 1999–2000 report illustrate the utility of the data (Vice Provost for Academic Affairs and Center for Quality and Planning, 2000, pp. 1–2).

> *Overall Satisfaction High.* Average satisfaction as measured on the survey's five-point scale was up slightly compared to last year (from 3.2 to 3.4). Both in the interviews and in written survey comments, exiting faculty continue to express positive views of the university. In many cases, departing faculty use phrases such as "wonderful," "a great university," "a good experience," and "I will miss it." Where feedback is mixed, positive general comments about the university often accompany a few specific negative comments. On balance, the respondents believe that the university is well managed and that they were treated fairly. They are proud of their affiliation with the university.

Child Care. The availability of child care is not, on average, a very important item to the faculty as a whole, but it is very important to some faculty members. This is an area where the university is making good progress. Satisfaction with child care has increased consistently from 1997–98 through 1999–2000, and this is true for all cohorts: male/female, junior/senior, and faculty at various locations.

Spousal Employment. Spousal employment is another issue that on average is not especially important to the faculty as a whole, but it is extremely relevant to some individuals. This continues to be a challenging area where attention is justified. Several exiting faculty members had comments similar to those of one individual. He said "the administration did make an honest, credible effort" to help his wife—and she did in fact get a professional position locally—but they decided to leave because her opportunities where simply much greater elsewhere.

In both the 1997–98 and 1998–99 studies, the climate, culture, practices, and processes for supporting junior faculty members, and the emphasis on and rewards for research (as opposed to teaching) were the two most prominent problem areas university-wide. In both cases, survey data and interview results continue to point to these as areas for potential improvement. Other important concerns are questions about the validity of faculty performance evaluations, and about whether rewards relate fairly to performance. Salary levels and salary increases also have been and remain problems.

This information is used in several ways. Every dean receives complete exit interview results for each participating faculty member in their respective colleges, with the permission of the individuals. This presents an opportunity to learn about and address situations within a college or department. The vice provost for academic affairs also presents a university-level report at a meeting of the institution's council of academic deans. This university holds three academic leadership forums every academic year for all department heads. About two-thirds of the department heads participate in a given year. One of the items for discussion at the academic leadership forums is information from the exit interview process. The goal is to improve understanding of faculty experiences, to raise awareness of what is working well and what is not, and to discuss possible improvements in communication, leadership, evaluation procedures, mentoring practices, and faculty development.

Faculty-Staff Surveys

Institutional research staff at this university also conduct an ongoing, long-term series of faculty-staff surveys. Approximately every five years, the university undertakes an institution-wide examination of faculty and staff's attitudes toward their jobs and the university as an employer. Most recently, a small sample telephone survey was conducted in 2000. At any time, any unit administrator, such as a college dean, can access a convenient follow-up survey for his or her own faculty and staff. These unit surveys can be tailored to the needs of a college, department, or division, and they are coordinated, administered, and analyzed by IR staff. The unit surveys are used because agendas for improvement and change are often best set at the level of work groups.

Part-Time and Full-Time Faculty

The use of part-time faculty in colleges and universities is a growing trend, one that generates criticism. The National Center for Education Statistics estimates that part-time instructors exceed 43 percent of the faculty and teach an estimated one-quarter of all courses and that the percentage of part-time faculty employed nearly doubled, from 22 percent to 41 percent, between 1970 and 1995 (cited in Balch, 1999). Many see this as a "regressive, unethical practice that strikes at the heart of academic quality" (Fulton, 2000, p. 39). Others argue that part-time faculty members are "highly committed and conscientious in their responsibilities, provide strong links to the community, and offer a wide variety of subject expertise at about one-third the cost of full-time instructors" (Balch, 1999, p. 33).

While debates continue about the merits of this trend, institutional research can shed some light on the matter for a given college or university. At the case study university, the factbook provided annual information on the distribution of faculty by appointment type and instructional productivity by various employment categories, such as regular faculty, part-time faculty, and graduate assistants. These data, however were scattered among several tables and in separate annual reports and were not sufficiently detailed to answer many questions. At the request of the faculty senate, already published available data were integrated and supplemented with previously unpublished but available information to produce a single report that provides longitudinal data on teaching by full-time and part-time faculty. That information is presented by appointment type, by rank, by gender, by college, and so on.

The report was first produced in 1999 and shared with the faculty senate. The data have been informative, and although the analysis was originally instigated by the senate, it is now also used by the university's senior leadership. One interesting finding—which surprised many in this university community—is that over the period covered to date (1992 through 1999), the proportion of teaching delivered by part-time faculty held steady at 18 percent of total student credit hours. However, the analysis also shows that the university coped with the dual pressures of enrollment growth and anemic state appropriations by maintaining the per-FTE teaching load of standing (tenured and tenure-track) faculty while almost doubling employment of and teaching by full-time but nonstanding (such as multiyear nontenure-track) faculty members. Over a seven-year period, student credit hour production by full-time nonstanding faculty rose from 11 percent to 21 percent of student credit hours. This change is much more marked in some high-demand rapid-growth departments or campuses of the university than others.

Equity Issues

Several targeted institutional research products have been created to address questions about whether the university's employees are treated fairly in terms of promotion opportunities and salary levels and increases. At the request of one of the university commissions for underrepresented groups, a new annual report was created in 1998 that uses an existing human resources database to examine time in rank for various faculty cohorts. This allows administrators and faculty members to make informed judgments about whether individuals from particular demographic groups, campuses, or colleges tend disproportionately to get stuck in the rank of associate professor. The same data allowed investigation of the "career assistant professor" phenomenon. Issues such as these matter because research universities operate in competitive national markets for faculty, so it is important to be as efficient and effective as possible in terms of faculty recruitment and retention. Also, questions about salary levels, promotion patterns, and demographic differences can be especially problematic if they involve potential equity issues.

Conclusions

Culture and norms have great power in colleges and universities, perhaps more than in most nonacademic organizations. It would be naive to expect important decisions affecting the management, enhancement, and development of faculty resources to be driven primarily by institutional research data. On the other hand, colleges and universities typically do have a great deal of data about their faculties, and often these data are underutilized. In the absence of accurate and well-presented institutional information, individual faculty members, faculty senates, provosts, deans, and department heads have little recourse but to base their attitudes and decisions on personal experience, anecdote, or assertions that may hold for higher education nationally but may not accurately describe local realities. This chapter illustrates specific ways institutional researchers can package data into information to support discussions, judgments, and decisions about faculty performance.

References

Balch, P. "Part-Time Faculty Are Here to Stay." *Planning for Higher Education,* 1999, 27(3), 32–41.

Birnbaum, R. "The Constraints on Campus Productivity." In R. E. Anderson and J. W. Meyerson (eds.), *Productivity and Higher Education*. Princeton, N.J.: Peterson's Guides, 1992.

Boyer, E. L. *Scholarship Reconsidered: Priorities of the Professoriate*. Princeton, N.J.: The Carnegie Foundation for the Advancement of Teaching, 1990.

Center for Quality and Planning. *Faculty Tenure Status: Distribution and Progression*. University Park, Penn.: Pennsylvania State University. Annual reports, 1998–2001.

Chait, R. "Why Academe Needs More Employment Options." *Chronicle of Higher Education*, Feb. 7, 1997, p. B4.

Cooke, A. *The Vintage Mencken*. New York: Vintage Press, 1958.

Fairweather, J. S. *Faculty Work and the Public Trust*. Boston: Allyn & Bacon, 1996.

Fulton, R. D. "The Plight of Part-Timers in Higher Education." *Change*, 2000, *32*(8), 38–43.

Glassick, C. E., Huber, M. T., and Maeroff, G. I. *Scholarship Assessed: Evaluation of the Professoriate*. San Francisco: Jossey-Bass, 1997.

Massy, W. F., and Zemsky, R. "Faculty Discretionary Time: Departments and the Academic Ratchet." *Journal of Higher Education*, 1994, *65*(1), 1–22.

Meyer, K. A. *Faculty Workload Studies: Perspectives, Needs, and Future Directions*. ASHE-ERIC Higher Education Research Report, vol. 26, no. 1. Washington, D.C.: Graduate School of Education and Human Development, George Washington University, 1998.

Middaugh, M. F., Trusheim, D. W., and Bauer, K. W. *Strategies for the Practice of Institutional Research: Concepts, Resources, and Applications*. Tallahassee, Fla.: Association for Institutional Research, 1994.

Rosovsky, H. Excerpts from Annual Report of the Dean of the Faculty of Arts and Sciences at Harvard University, 1990–91. *Pew Policy Perspectives*, 1992, *4*(3), 1b–2b.

Sax, L. J., and others. *The American College Teacher: National Norms for the 1998–99 HERI Faculty Survey*. Los Angeles: Higher Education Research Institute, UCLA, 1999.

Terenzini, P. T. "On the Nature of Institutional Research and the Knowledge and Skills It Requires." In J. F. Volkwein (ed.), *What Is Institutional Research All About? A Critical and Comprehensive Assessment of the Profession*. New Directions for Institutional Research, no. 104. San Francisco: Jossey-Bass, 1999.

Vice Provost for Academic Affairs and Center for Quality and Planning. *1999–2000 Faculty Exit Study: Analysis of Responses*. University Park, Penn.: Pennsylvania State University, Aug. 2000.

Volkwein, J. F. (ed.). *What Is Institutional Research All About? A Critical and Comprehensive Assessment of the Profession*. New Directions for Institutional Research, no. 104. San Francisco: Jossey-Bass, 1999.

Wergin, J. F. (ed.). *Analyzing Faculty Workload*. New Directions for Institutional Research, no. 83. San Francisco: Jossey-Bass, 1994.

Whitely, M. A., Porter, J. D., and Fenske, R. H. *The Primer for Institutional Research*. (Rev. ed.). Tallahassee, Fla.: Association for Institutional Research, 1992.

MICHAEL J. DOORIS is director of planning research and assessment in the Center for Quality and Planning and a member of the graduate faculty in higher education at Pennsylvania State University.

This chapter translates the recommendations made by the previous authors to inform departmental and college personnel decisions, particularly promotion and tenure.

The Ultimate Faculty Evaluation: Promotion and Tenure Decisions

James S. Fairweather

In this chapter I take the perspective of the former chair and current member of the College Reappointment, Promotion, and Tenure Committee (RPT) in the College of Education at Michigan State University (MSU). Based on this experience and many others (see Fairweather, 1996), I conclude that the faculty in our college draw inferences about what their institution, college, and department value the most by viewing the outcome of promotion and tenure decisions (and sometimes salaries and raises) more than by the ways that a college or institution chooses to measure performance and set RPT criteria. As Huber notes in Chapter Seven, "*scholarship* gains specific meaning less in rules and regulations than in deliberations about particular cases." Particularly important is the distinction between goal clarification and the measurement of performance, on the one hand, and assigning value to distinct aspects of a faculty member's performance in a RPT decision, on the other. The former assist an RPT committee in understanding what a faculty member accomplished; they do not help us decide how to value the different accomplishments nor do they tell us whether or not the overall record is sufficient to achieve promotion or tenure. Ultimately, RPT decisions rest on values and judgments, not on measurement or clear expectations. Missions and philosophy help shape an institutional culture; the translation of missions and philosophy into practice is what matters in RPT decisions. In this context, the preceding chapters inform personnel decisions primarily by defining and assessing the components of faculty work. Left unaddressed are the value judgments inherent in the process, which I explore in this chapter.

NEW DIRECTIONS FOR INSTITUTIONAL RESEARCH, no. 114, Summer 2002 © Wiley Periodicals, Inc.

Recommendations for Good Practice

In this section, I examine assumptions about the nature of the faculty position, components of faculty work examined in RPT decisions, and distinctions between evaluation designed for research and evaluation designed to assist decision making.

Assumptions About the Faculty Position. The previous chapters focus primarily on full-time tenure-track faculty with the assumption that all aspects of faculty work, even if reconfigured or defined differently, should be reflected in the work of each faculty member. Hence the complexity of evaluation lies in understanding and making sense of each component of faculty work.

This assumption is only partly correct. Gappa and Leslie (1993) and Baldwin and Chronister (2000) show that almost one-half of college teaching at four-year institutions is carried out by part-time or non-tenure-track faculty members. Geiger (1990) demonstrates that many colleges and universities hire non-tenure-track faculty to carry out research. The success of land grant universities in providing public service lies in part because they created extension programs with their own staffs rather than relying on regular faculty members (Lynton and Elman, 1987).

I do not quarrel with the focus on full-time, tenure-track faculty members. Improving the evaluation of regular faculty members surely can lead to improved productivity across the range of faculty work. My point is that some *collective goals* or responsibilities of the organizational unit (program, department, or college) might be better resolved by using alternative staff rather than by changing assessment procedures or reconfiguring faculty work. Karen Paulson (2002) argues that the effectiveness of technology-based instruction is enhanced by unbundling disciplinary expertise from the delivery of instruction, which may be better suited for professionals trained in the use of technology. Evaluation of teaching quality must include the large portion of undergraduate instruction provided by teaching assistants, part-timers, and non-tenure-track faculty. Some scholarship of application might be better achieved by staff in technology transfer units than by faculty in traditional academic departments (Fairweather, 1996). Staff other than faculty may be better prepared to work with local high schools to encourage students to take the mathematics and science courses they will need to become engineers. In sum, efforts to improve teaching, research, and service by improving the evaluation of tenure-track faculty can only be partially successful because many departments and colleges carry out their collective goals by using non-tenure-track faculty and teaching assistants along with full-time faculty members.

The Components of Faculty Work. In the following, I summarize the measurement and evaluation recommendations made in previous chapters by category of faculty work.

Instruction. Paulsen (Chapter One) recommends that the evaluation of instruction start by distinguishing its different parts, including classroom teaching, advising, and dissertation committee work. He also recommends examining faculty contributions to out-of-class learning experiences, which can affect the cognitive and social development of students (Pascarella and Terenzini, 1991). Then, Paulsen recommends going far beyond the traditional measures of teaching performance, such as student ratings of instructional performance. He argues persuasively that portfolios give more accurate assessments of teaching performance when they include evidence of active and collaborative instruction, peer review of classroom instruction, innovative forms of student assessment, and longitudinal tracking of student progress. Paulsen's emphasis on the intermediate indicators of eventual student learning, such as the use of active and collaborative teaching in the classroom, seems the easiest of these recommendations to adopt in the RPT decision-making process.

Research and Scholarship. Braxton and Del Favero (Chapter Two) propose a new template to assess scholarship based on Boyer's *Scholarship Reconsidered* (1990). The new template emphasizes the scholarships of discovery (that is, traditional scholarship), application, integration, and teaching. They argue against a "one size fits all" model. To encourage academic leaders to adopt this new template, Braxton and Del Favero present several types of assessment, each with specific measures. They imply that using their scheme will help academic institutions adopt rewards more consistent with these broader definitions of scholarship. I found most useful their recommendation to identify the major research and teaching-oriented journals in each discipline and use them to help assess scholarly productivity. Less convincing is their reliance on citation indices and other types of scores (see Mary Frank Fox, 1985, for a discussion of the strengths and weaknesses of citation indices). Braxton and Del Favero believe that the change in evaluation template and associated measures will transform rewards.

Scholarship of Teaching. Huber (Chapter Seven) advocates the scholarship of teaching as a special category of faculty work. Huber distinguishes scholarly teaching (improving one's teaching through observation and assessment) from the scholarship of teaching (disseminating research about teaching in peer-reviewed outlets). As I discuss later, the application of the scholarship of teaching in RPT decisions is less satisfactory than Huber's discussion of the concepts, in part because these distinctions are not clear in practice. Moreover, clarifying the definition and measurement of the scholarship of teaching cannot lead to its successful application in RPT decisions without concomitant consensus about its value as a faculty activity.

Service. Amey (Chapter Three) emphasizes the use of portfolios to document faculty contributions to service. She takes care to distinguish administrative from national service, outreach to the public from serving on university committees. Amey sees decisions to promote systemic reform and institutional transformation as preceding (or at least concomitant with) changing the assessment of faculty work. Amey recommends that the weight given to service productivity be consistent with institutional mission, although neither she nor the other authors tell us how to achieve this goal.

The Total Job. Instead of emphasizing distinct parts of the faculty job, Colbeck (Chapter Four) stresses integration of faculty work across categories. As an example, she defines coauthoring a publication with a student as evidence of both research productivity and effective teaching (as a contribution to student professional development). Her perspective is the most consistent with RPT decisions, which must take into account a faculty member's total contribution.

Usefulness for Research Is Not Equivalent to Usefulness in Decision Making. As a researcher studying faculty work, I found each of these chapters valuable. Braxton and Del Favero, Paulsen, Amey, Colbeck, and Huber all provide important clues for how to construct measures of active and collaborative instruction, public service, the overlap of teaching and research productivity, and distinct types of scholarly output from national and institutional data sources. Although recommendations for the use of portfolio assessment, peer review, and other innovative approaches seem potentially quite useful when considered one at a time, their cumulative effect on faculty work and their application in RPT decision making is more problematic. Portfolios, peer review, and external review are labor-intensive activities. Adopting some or all of these approaches may make it difficult for faculty members to improve the very practices these assessment forms are meant to address. In another venue (Fairweather, 1993), I have shown that when faculty members spend more time on one activity they usually spend less time on another. Will the extra hours preparing portfolios come out of the time a faculty member would otherwise have spent on learning to be a better teacher, on community outreach, or on publishing? What will be the net costs and benefits? We need a systems perspective here for how the various recommended new forms of assessment will be incorporated in the faculty job. Dooris (Chapter Eight) recognizes that some assessments are not worth the cost regardless of their intellectual appeal.

The various proposals to increase the amount and type of evaluation runs counter to our experience at Michigan State University. In the College of Education RPT Committee, we have found that *reducing* the material in the RPT folders, not increasing it, improves decisions. Asking candidates for promotion or tenure to select their three best publications for review has meant that all RPT committee members will read the materials and be able to discuss the intellectual contributions of published work. In the past, we were often overwhelmed by the volume of information. Individual committee members often read different parts of the dossier. Without question, using a more concise set of evaluation measures makes for a more reasoned and accurate decision. Simply adding innovative forms of evaluation will not improve decision making. To be effective, the recommendations made in this volume must be placed in the context of the personnel decision process. What counts is understanding how the decision process works and what data are likely to improve decisions.

The RPT Decision

In this section, I discuss the importance of goal setting, direction, and history in establishing RPT criteria. Next, I discuss the various decisions about faculty work and the consequences for evaluation. Finally, I discuss the dynamics of the RPT decision.

Goal Setting, Direction, and History. The intent of RPT is to incorporate institutional (or college or departmental) priorities into the personnel decision-making process. Whether explicitly or not, the evaluation of faculty performance incorporates *values* about the relative importance of faculty work and unit goals. The typical rotating pattern of faculty participation in RPT committees and accompanying loss of institutional memory make consistent values judgments problematic. Other complications include lack of communication about intent and variation in expectations and performance between department and college.

The changes in evaluating faculty work recommended by previous chapter authors can assist in transforming institutions when two crucial parts of the transformation process are included. The first, discussed in a later section, is that some communication and agreement about the goals of the institution, college, and department between relevant administrators and their faculties must either precede or accompany changes in evaluation of faculty members. The second is that understanding the history of the program or department, college, or institution must precede setting targets for changes needed to advance those goals.

Examples to Consider. Despite being in a major research university, the College of Education at MSU has a long-standing commitment to excellence in teaching and outreach. Any imbalance in faculty productivity shows up in lack of traditional scholarship and funded research, not in poor-quality teaching or lack of outreach. Similarly, Carol Colbeck, Andrea Beach, and I (Fairweather and Beach, 2000) found wide variation in commitment to and expectations for research, teaching, and service between and within research universities. For example, the University of Tennessee–Knoxville (UTK) has a strong historical commitment to teaching. UTK's research university status depends on high levels of research productivity in a handful of departments, such as physics. Developing a faculty evaluation strategy to encourage greater commitment to teaching may make sense in the UTK physics department. This approach seems redundant and possibly counterproductive in many other UTK departments. Understanding current strengths and weaknesses in an academic unit is fundamental to identifying goals that guide changes in faculty evaluation strategies. Without this a priori assessment, adopting new measures for assessing teaching effectiveness or research productivity may unintentionally lead the academic unit in the wrong direction.

The Current Personnel Decision Process. Paulsen (Chapter One) correctly calls for academic leaders to make expectations for faculty work explicit. Too often junior faculty must figure out the relative importance of criteria by themselves (Boice, 1992), an inefficient trial-and-error process with no guarantee that junior faculty will "get it right." Amey (Chapter Three) correctly views the RPT decision and other types of faculty evaluation as part of a larger system. Making performance criteria explicit requires that both the faculty members under review and those conducting the review understand formal and informal parts of this system. In some institutions and colleges, the RPT committee vote becomes a formal part of the faculty member's dossier. In others, the role of the RPT committee is advisory to the dean, whose vote is the only official assessment entered into the dossier. In many prestigious colleges and universities, the RPT committee vote may be more important than the vote of any administrator. Each scenario involves the department chair, dean, and RPT committee differently. The agent responsible for making criteria clear and the appropriate source of information about criteria may differ depending on the decision-making process.

Translating Philosophy and Intent into Personnel Decisions. Earlier chapters effectively portray measurement options for evaluating faculty work. Amey, for example, distinguishes between effective outreach and good citizenship. Colbeck (Chapter Four) provides a general framework for evaluating faculty work arguing that evaluation should consider the "entire scope of faculty work" rather than its distinct parts. Braxton and Del Favero (Chapter Two) want the evaluation system to reflect institutional values and to account for the variation by discipline and program. Huber (Chapter Seven) explores the scholarship of teaching, expanding the target audience to include non-tenure-track faculty members. Missing from all of these recommendations is how to translate philosophy and mission into practice, especially making personnel decisions.

Consider outreach in more detail. Consistent with Amey's perspective, MSU has revised the RPT criteria to include several outreach subcategories of service and provides examples of how to measure these subcategories. MSU even goes so far as to bring Colbeck's perspective into the process, saying that RPT committees should attend to how outreach activities affect teaching and research. Yet, specification of guidelines and clarification of definitions and measures do not tell me as an RPT Committee member how to value the different types of contributions within a category of performance (such as serving on university committees versus performing community outreach) or between categories (such as outreach and research). *Measuring* the outcome of an activity enhances its visibility but does not give it *value* in making a decision about reappointment, promotion, and tenure.

Values Are Reflected in Judgments, Not Measurements. At its heart, the RPT decision process consists of individuals working together to make a professional judgment about a faculty member's performance. This judgment reflects the values of both the reviewers and those being reviewed as an explicit part of the decision process or implicitly by relying on the decision(s) to influence the values of other faculty members. Placing information in a particular format, however well defined, may rationalize the process but it will not help RPT committee members judge the relative importance of different faculty achievements. Nor is this rationality a substitute for an honest appraisal of the strengths and weaknesses of a department or college and the faculty achievements that should be weighted most heavily to improve the performance of the relevant organizational unit. We can expand the definition of *scholarship* by using Braxton and Del Favero's scheme, but the scheme alone will not inform RPT committees how to value the different types of scholarship relative to other faculty achievements. We can include teaching-oriented journals in RPT materials, but to be effective, RPT committee members must value or give weight to publications in these journals. As Dooris (Chapter Eight) implies, documenting the results of RPT decisions tells institutional leaders what happened but does not tell them what should have happened.

Outcomes of Faculty Evaluation

The potential effectiveness of evaluation strategies depends in part on the desired outcome. Ensuring *accountability* requires different measures and standards than do assessments of *quality* and *impact*. The former might emphasize the number of courses taught and student credit hours generated, whereas the latter might examine instructional approaches and student learning outcomes. Accountability often emphasizes local norms such as teaching and service more than national ones such as research and scholarship (Alpert, 1985). Measures of accountability are easier to develop than measures of impact or quality because the latter focus on more ephemeral goals (for example, student learning, impact of research) and contain implicit values.

RPT decisions focus more on quality and impact than on accountability, although citizenship and work load can influence the decision. All RPT decisions are not the same. Reappointment, tenure (with promotion to associate professor), and promotion to full professor are distinct outcomes. Although RPT committees consider similar measures of performance for all three decisions, the relative importance of and standards for distinct achievements differs.

Many, perhaps most, institutions today have annual faculty reviews. These reviews can include measures of both accountability and impact that affect merit pay increases. Often these reviews are included in RPT dossiers but do not incorporate the longitudinal perspective of promotion and tenure deliberations. Posttenure review is an extension of the annual review, perhaps done less frequently, with a focus on accountability and continued productivity (Licata, 1986).

Evaluation has another connotation. Sorcinelli and Austin (1992) emphasize the importance of assessing faculty performance to encourage professional development. Here the evaluation is not meant to demonstrate performance but to identify shortcomings and help the faculty member become more effective.

Complexity of Personnel Decision Making

Evaluation of faculty performance, particularly RPT decisions, is made complex by the difficulty in measuring outcomes and the need to achieve some consensus about their relative importance. Even more complex is the need to assure that both individual and collective goals and responsibilities are met. In my experience, the most difficult task in evaluating faculty performance is simultaneously being fair to the individual faculty member while promoting the health of the academic unit. In the following, I describe two promotion and tenure scenarios, both at the tenure/associate professor decision level, that demonstrate complexity of and potential conflict between the individual and the organization. Both scenarios reflect real experiences, although I have changed the specifics to preserve confidentiality.

Scenario 1. Candidates A and B—both women—come up for tenure at the same time in the MSU College of Education. Both work in departments with a strong commitment to practice. Candidate A works in a department divided informally into two camps that are both on the tenure track, the researcher/scholars and the practitioners. The practitioners carry a higher teaching and service load than do the researchers but are expected to carry out modest levels of research. This departmental expectation for scholarly productivity is neither shared across the college nor made explicit in departmental policy. Candidate A falls into the practitioner camp.

In contrast, Candidate B works in a department where each individual is expected to "do it all." Her department does not distinguish between practitioners and researcher/scholars. The expected level and type of scholarly productivity is consistent with stated college guidelines.

In reviewing the respective dossiers, the RPT Committee found Candidate A to have excellent teaching and service records. Less clear was her scholarly productivity, which claimed to fit the scholarship of teaching. The candidate had few refereed articles or other forms of national dissemination. Publications were based on the candidate's own classroom experience and published in minor journals. Supporting letters indicated that the departmental review committee and the chair believed her record, including the level and type of scholarly productivity, was sufficient to justify tenure.

Now we turn to Candidate B. The RPT Committee found Candidate B's teaching and service record every bit as compelling as Candidate A's record. In addition, Candidate B's scholarly record combined refereed publications in top journals, with articles in applied journals and a major research grant. The dossier included letters of support from the departmental committee and the chair on par with those for Candidate A.

The RPT Committee had no difficulty in recommending tenure and promotion for Candidate B. The resolution for Candidate A was problematic. Although I will not reveal the decision, I will describe the dynamics and complexity involved. Candidate A appeared to respond to the expressed collective needs of her department. Her teaching and service records were exemplary. According to the department, she met the minimal expectations for research. Yet her record neither met the stated collegewide expectations for research nor did it compare favorably with Candidate B. In this case, what do we mean by fairness to the individual and to the collective? If the RPT Committee denied tenure to Candidate A, were we being unfair to an individual who met the (admittedly unstated) expectations of her department? Would we be unfair to Candidate B if we were to judge Candidate A solely on the basis of departmental expectations? Would we be telling Candidate B that she would not have had to achieve highly in all categories of faculty work if she had been a member of Candidate A's department?

The collective needs of the college include promoting scholarship and funded research, whereas the collective needs of Candidate A's department focus on preparing practitioners. If the RPT Committee voted to tenure Candidate A on the basis of helping her department achieve its goals, how would that affect college-wide goals? If College RPT decisions promote local norms (teaching and service) at the expense of national norms (research and scholarship) will the college end up over time with a faculty having little stature nationally? If the RPT committee does not pay sufficient attention to local needs, will departments fail to achieve teaching and service objectives?

Scenario 2. In another college at MSU as part of an accreditation process, the RPT Committee was asked to review the annual performance of faculty in a specific department. The committee found that each faculty member in the department made satisfactory contributions in each category of faculty work. Yet the evaluation criteria for individual faculty members omitted key collective responsibilities, such as curriculum reform and recruiting students. The accreditation site-visit team rated the department lower than expected because it failed to fulfill these collective responsibilities. This scenario reveals that even when all faculty members in a department produce adequately in the stated performance categories, some collective responsibilities can still be neglected (Fisher, Fairweather, and Amey, 2001).

Careful specification and measurement of faculty performance across activities called for in this volume can provide important information in faculty personnel decisions. Yet these clarifications alone have not helped the RPT Committee make a decision in either scenario. The scenarios point out the need to reach agreement at the institutional, college, and department levels about what should count in faculty work.

Choosing and Conveying Values

We academics most commonly convey values about academic work by leaving it to individual faculty members to draw their own conclusions based on promotion and tenure decisions. This informal method of communication is inefficient and can be misleading. Consider Scenario 1 discussed previously. If the RPT Committee denied Candidate A's request for tenure because she did not meet a minimum level of collegewide research productivity and because of concerns about fairness to Candidate B and others like her, other faculty members in the college might conclude that teaching and service, the mainstays of Candidate A's case, do not count in promotion and tenure. Alternatively, if the RPT Committee recommended that tenure be granted to Candidate A because of her contributions to the collective goals of the department, other college faculty members might conclude that research does not really matter or that tenure and promotion are influenced by the size and visibility of one's department rather than by one's productivity. None of these interpretations would be accurate. All would serve to divide faculty into competing camps.

Far better, in my view, is to have ongoing conversations among the faculty, among administrators at various levels, and between faculty and administrators about the relative importance of faculty achievements. I am not arguing here that administrators set hard-and-fast guidelines or micromanage the RPT decision process. Faculty on RPT committees need some degree of freedom to judge the balance of faculty achievements to assess what Colbeck calls the "whole of faculty work." I am arguing that the process of forming collective understanding about the value of faculty work, however difficult and messy, is preferable and more effective in improving faculty productivity and in meeting collective and individual objectives than relying on the decisions to convey these messages. Perhaps RPT committees might help forge a consensus among the faculty and administrators in their respective colleges (or other relevant organizational level) by using particular cases or scenarios to demonstrate the values imbedded in the choices they must make. An open discussion about the various choices and what they would mean for individuals, programs, departments, and colleges can only be healthy.

Huber notes that a trend in academe is to increase expectations for performance by each individual faculty member, resulting in high levels of stress and conceivably reducing performance. An important policy question is whether all aspects of faculty work should be part of each individual faculty member's dossier. Why add outreach as an expectation for a faculty member if professional staff are better suited to the task? Or why not limit expectations for outreach contributions to activities faculty members seem best suited to carry out? Is it efficient and effective for colleges to expect their faculty members to use technology effectively in instruction? If so, what parts of instruction—course development, Web-based delivery, assessment, or content—should be evaluated? (See McInnis, Chapter Five; Marine, Chapter Six.) If most faculty members focus on the scholarship of teaching consistent with their teaching and service obligations, what will happen to the scholarship of discovery? Evaluation, identifying the important parts of faculty work and finding ways to measure them, is a necessary but not sufficient step in answering these difficult value questions.

Defining collective responsibilities is crucial. Implicit in many of the chapter authors' recommendations is that the current methods of evaluating faculty work do not adequately address some department, college, or institutional obligations. I agree. It is ineffective, in my opinion, to redress these shortcomings by simply expanding expectations for individual faculty performance. Instead, key policy questions include who should be doing what, whether tenure-track faculty members are the relevant group to carry out all collective obligations, and what different types of performance across categories of work meet both individual and collective objectives. In the end, making these value judgments and basing policy on them is the foundation for all effective forms of faculty evaluation.

References

Alpert, D. "Performance and Paralysis: The Organizational Context of the American Research University." *Journal of Higher Education,* 1985, 56, 241–281.

Baldwin, R., and Chronister, J. *Teaching Without Tenure: Policies and Practices for a New Era.* Baltimore: Johns Hopkins University Press, 2000.

Boice, R. *The New Faculty Member.* San Francisco: Jossey-Bass, 1992.

Boyer, E. L. *Scholarship Reconsidered: Priorities of the Professoriate.* Princeton, N.J.: The Carnegie Foundation for the Advancement of Teaching, 1990.

Fairweather, J. "Faculty Rewards Reconsidered: The Nature of Tradeoffs." *Change,* 1993, 25, 44–47.

Fairweather, J. *Faculty Work and Public Trust: Restoring the Value of Teaching and Public Service in American Academic Life.* Boston: Allyn & Bacon, 1996.

Fairweather, J., and Beach, A. "Variation in Faculty Work Within Research Universities: Policy Implications for Achieving Balance Between Teaching, Research, and Service." Paper presented at the annual meeting of the Association for the Study of Higher Education, Sacramento, Nov. 2000.

Fisher, P., Fairweather, J., and Amey, M. "Systemic Reform in Undergraduate Engineering Education: The Role of Collective Responsibility." Paper presented at Frontiers in Education Conference, Reno, Oct. 2001.

Fox, M. F. "Publication, Performance, and Reward in Science and Scholarship." In J. Smart (ed.), *Higher Education: Handbook of Theory and Research.* Vol. 1. New York: Agathon Press, 1985.

Gappa, J., and Leslie, D. *The Invisible Faculty: Improving the Status of Part-Timers in Higher Education.* San Francisco: Jossey-Bass, 1993.

Geiger, R. "Organized Research Units: Their Role in the Development of University Research." *Journal of Higher Education,* 1990, 61, 1–19.

Licata, C. *Post-tenure Faculty Evaluation: Threat or Opportunity?* ASHE-ERIC Higher Education Research Report, no. 1. Washington, D.C.: Association for the Study of Higher Education, 1986.

Lynton, E., and Elman, S. *New Priorities for the University.* San Francisco: Jossey-Bass, 1987.

Pascarella, E., and Terenzini, P. *How College Affects Students.* San Francisco: Jossey-Bass, 1991.

Paulson, K. "Reconfiguring Faculty Roles in Virtual Settings." *Journal of Higher Education,* 2002, 73(1), 123–131.

Sorcinelli, M., and Austin, A. (eds.). *Developing New and Junior Faculty.* New Directions for Teaching and Learning, no. 50. San Francisco: Jossey-Bass, 1992.

JAMES S. FAIRWEATHER is professor of higher, adult and lifelong education at Michigan State University and nationally known for his work in faculty roles and rewards, industry-university partnerships, reforming undergraduate engineering education, and higher education policy.

INDEX

Back Issue/Subscription Order Form

Copy or detach and send to:
Jossey-Bass, A Wiley Company, 989 Market Street, San Francisco CA 94103-1741

Call or fax toll-free: Phone 888-378-2537 6:30AM – 3PM PST; Fax 888-481-2665

Back Issues: Please send me the following issues at $27 each
(Important: please include ISBN number with your order.)

_____

_____

_____

$ _____   Total for single issues

$ _____   SHIPPING CHARGES: SURFACE   Domestic Canadian

First Item	$5.00	$6.00
Each Add'l Item	$3.00	$1.50

For next-day and second-day delivery rates, call the number listed above.

Subscriptions   Please ❏ start ❏ renew my subscription to *New Directions for Institutional Research* for the year 2_____at the following rate:

U.S.	❏ Individual $65	❏ Institutional $125
Canada	❏ Individual $65	❏ Institutional $165
All Others	❏ Individual $89	❏ Institutional $199
Online Subscription		❏ Institutional $125

**For more information about online subscriptions visit
www.interscience.wiley.com**

$ _____   Total single issues and subscriptions (Add appropriate sales tax for your state for single issue orders. No sales tax for U.S. subscriptions. Canadian residents, add GST for subscriptions and single issues.)

❏Payment enclosed (U.S. check or money order only)
❏VISA ❏ MC ❏ AmEx ❏ Discover Card #_____ Exp. Date _____

Signature _____ Day Phone _____
❏ Bill Me (U.S. institutional orders only. Purchase order required.)

Purchase order # _____
      Federal Tax ID13559302   **GST 89102 8052**

Name _____

Address _____

_____

Phone _____ E-mail _____

For more information about Jossey-Bass, visit our Web site at www.josseybass.com

PROMOTION CODE ND3

intelligence that make up IR—technical/analytical, contextual, and issues intelligence.
ISBN: 0-7879-1406-1

IR103   **How Technology Is Changing Institutional Research**
Liz Sanders
Illustrates how to streamline office functions through the use of new technologies, assesses the impact of distance learning on faculty workload and student learning, and responds to the new opportunities and problems posed by expanding information access.
ISBN: 0-7879-5240-0

IR102   **Information Technology in Higher Education: Assessing Its Impact and Planning for the Future**
Richard N. Katz, Julia A. Rudy
Provides campus leaders, institutional researchers, and information technologists much-needed guidance for determining how IT investments should be made, measured, and assessed. Offers practical, effective models for integrating IT planning into institutional planning and goals, assessing the impact of IT investments on teaching, learning, and administrative operations, and promoting efficient information management practices.
ISBN: 0-7879-1409-6

IR101   **A New Era of Alumni Research: Improving Institutional Performance and Better Serving Alumni**
Joseph Pettit, Larry L. Litten
Drawing from information generated by mail and telephone surveys, focus groups, and institutional data analysis, the authors examine various facets of an institution's relationship with alumni—including fundraising from alumni, services for alumni, and occupational and other outcomes of college.
ISBN: 0-7879-1407-X

IR100   **Using Teams in Higher Education: Cultural Foundations for Productive Change**
Susan H. Frost
Using research and practice from higher education, where teams are used with varying degrees of effectiveness, and from business, where teams are linked to survival, this issue addresses questions of culture, especially as they can affect significant aspects of teamwork. Explores the theory and practice related to different types of teams and the dynamics that influence success.
ISBN: 0-7879-1415-0

IR99   **Quality Assurance in Higher Education: An International Perspective**
Gerald H. Gaither
Offers an international set of resources—including Web sites and other electronic resources—to assist practitioners in achieving the goals of their own quality assurance frameworks.
ISBN: 0-7879-4740-7

IR98   **Campus Climate: Understanding the Critical Components of Today's Colleges and Universities**
Karen W. Bauer
Provides guidelines for effective assessment of today's diverse campus populations, highlighting key diversity issues that affect women, racial and ethnic minorities; and lesbian, gay, bisexual, transgender, and disabled students.
ISBN: 0-78791416-9

information that will help them to understand changing student needs; facilitate and assess student learning; assess and understand faculty culture; and redefine, assign, and assess faculty work.
ISBN: 0-7879-9989-X

IR83   **Analyzing Faculty Workload**
Jon F. Wergin
Explores how the public discourse about faculty work might be improved and suggests how colleges and universities might document that work in a fashion that not only more faithfully describes what faculty do but also allows for reports that are more comprehensive and useful.
ISBN: 0-7879-9988-1

IR82   **Using Performance Indicators to Guide Strategic Decision Making**
Victor M. H. Borden, Trudy W. Banta
The goal of this issue is threefold: to provide the reader with an understanding of what has led to the current popularity of indicator systems; to illustrate several possible methods for developing performance indicators; and to synthesize theory and practice into a formulation for a proactive, institution-based approach to indicator development.
ISBN: 0-7879-9964-4

IR78   **Pursuit of Quality in Higher Education: Case Studies in Total Quality Management**
Deborah J. Teeter, G. Gregory Lozier
Provides valuable insights into the experiences of colleges and universities that are applying the principles of Total Quality Management (TQM) to higher education. Presents different aspects of TQM regarding issues of organization, training, use of tools or methodologies, the language of TQM, or the challenges in transforming organizational cultures.
ISBN: 1-55542-693-X

IR66   **Organizing Effective Institutional Research Offices**
Jennifer B. Presley
Designed to assist both those who are establishing an institutional research function for the first time and those who are invigorating an existing unit. Provides major guidelines for how to approach tasks and avoid major pitfalls.
ISBN: 1-55542-829-0

IR61   **Planning and Managing Higher Education Facilities**
Harvey H. Kaiser
Provides information on facilities management for institutional researchers, with theories and application covering a range of topics from a global perspective to specific issues.
ISBN: 1-55542-868-1

IR55   **Managing Information in Higher Education**
E. Michael Staman
Describes many of the key elements in the development of an information management program and the policies and procedures that must be in place if the program is to be successful and sustainable over time.
ISBN: 1-55542-947-5